Conjoint Behavioral Consultation

A Procedural Manual

APPLIED CLINICAL PSYCHOLOGY

Series Editors:
Alan S. Bellack
University of Maryland at Baltimore, Baltimore, Maryland
Michel Hersen
Nova Southeastern University, Fort Lauderdale, Florida

Current volumes in this Series

A Continuation Order Plan is available for this series. A continuation order will bring delivery of each new volume immediately upon publication. Volumes are billed only upon actual shipment. For further information please contact the publisher.

Conjoint Behavioral Consultation
A Procedural Manual

Susan M. Sheridan
University of Utah
Salt Lake City, Utah

Thomas R. Kratochwill
University of Wisconsin–Madison
Madison, Wisconsin

and

John R. Bergan
University of Arizona
Tuscon, Arizona

Plenum Press • New York and London

Library of Congress Cataloging-in-Publication Data

Sheridan, Susan M.
    Conjoint behavioral consultation : a procedural manual / Susan M.
Sheridan, Thomas R. Kratochwill, and John R. Bergan.
        p. cm. -- (Applied clinical psychology)
    Includes bibliographical references and index.
    ISBN 0-306-45155-7
    1. Mental health consultation. 2. Behavioral assessment of
children. 3. School psychology. I. Kratochwill, Thomas R.
II. Bergan, John R., 1931- . III. Title. IV. Series.
RJ503.45.S54 1996
618.92'89--dc20   95-46987
                                                                       CIP

ISBN 0-306-45155-7

© 1996 Plenum Press, New York
A Division of Plenum Publishing Corporation
233 Spring Street, New York, N. Y. 10013

10 9 8 7 6 5 4 3 2 1

Printed in the United States of America

To Jack and Carol Sheridan for their ongoing love and support, to the loving memory of Marian F. Kratochwill, and to Kathy, John, and David Bergan

Preface

This book is intended to provide a procedural guide for the practice of conjoint behavioral consultation. It is a guide for practitioners, clinicians, students, and trainers who are interested in extending their consultation work to include more than one consultee and more than one system in the problem-solving process. An overview of the model and research findings are also included to provide a broad perspective of work in this area. Finally, actual case studies are included to embellish the description of the model and illustrate its utility with a number of presenting difficulties.

This guide is not meant to provide extensive background about consultation practice and research. As an extension of behavioral consultation, it assumes that readers are knowledgeable about basic procedures and practice issues. Although Chapter 1 reviews behavioral consultation stages, this overview is not sufficient to ensure that readers possess adequate skills to engage in the practice. Rather, this book is best used to complement Bergan and Kratochwill's *Behavioral Consultation and Therapy* (1990) and Kratochwill and Bergan's *Behavioral Consultation in Applied Settings: An Individual Guide* (1990). All of these works are also meant to supplement, not replace, a comprehensive training program. Such a program typically takes place over several months and encompasses competency-based knowledge and skill training, applied practical components, and ongoing supervision. With such procedures, the full benefits of this guide can be realized.

Each chapter in this book begins with a statement of chapter objectives and ends with a list of discussion questions. It is recommended that readers take time to consider these features carefully and to use them as guides by which to assure understanding of key points. Likewise, the interview guides presented in the Appendix serve as tools for moving through conjoint behavioral consultation interviews. If possible, it is strongly recommended that individuals engage in practice activities and obtain feedback on performance objectives. The use of audiotape cassette recorders may be invaluable to self-monitor one's own performance and to structure supervision sessions. In any event, learning the model is an ongoing process; performance seems to improve over time with practice, feedback, and experience.

The procedures presented in this guide must be recognized as tools to assist clinicians, practitioners, and students in conducting consultation cases. The effectiveness of consultation services is affected by numerous variables, only some of which concern the standardized procedures presented herein. Users of this guide are advised to remember that consultation represents an ongoing process that is often mediated by factors such as interpersonal skills, relationship dynamics, problem severity, willingness of participants, competencies of consultees and clients, and many other issues. Clearly, consultation takes place in a relationship that is sometimes complex and complicated. The procedures offer a guide by which to embark upon and move through the consultation stages, but these procedures must be considered in the context of these other interacting variables.

Acknowledgments

We would like to thank several individuals who have worked with us over the years to help in the conceptualization and development of the conjoint behavioral consultation model. We also appreciate many persons who have contributed to the research in this area and who assisted in the completion of this guide. In particular, we are grateful to Stephen N. Elliott, Bill Erchul, Randy Busse, Denise Colton, Jason Feld, JoAnn Galloway, Kevin Fenstermacher, Pam Loitz, Sherry Robertson-Mjaanes, Ingrid Sladeczek, Murline Steck, and Melissa Twernbold. We acknowledge Karen O'Connell for her assistance in word processing the manuscript and Ryan Gothard for his assistance in graphics. We are also indebted to the many teachers, parents, and children who have served as participants in consultation and from whom we have learned a great deal.

Contents

Behavioral Consultation
Introduction and Research

Upon completing this chapter, the reader should be able to:

1. Provide at least three rationales for consultation services.
2. Outline the primary characteristics of behavioral consultation.
3. Identify the participants and their roles in behavioral consultation.
4. List the stages of behavioral consultation.
5. Discuss objectives of each behavioral consultation stage.
6. Define the following terms:
   - operational definition
   - goal specification
   - antecedent, consequent, and sequential conditions
   - skill and performance deficits
   - treatment acceptability
7. Review general research findings regarding behavioral consultation.

Consultation is a form of service delivery that is gaining increased recognition in research, training, and practice. In consultation, two or more persons work together to address concerns regarding a third-party client. Of the several theoretical models of consultation described in the psychological and educational literature, behavioral consultation has received the greatest amount of research attention and some empirical support. Several reviews of the consultation literature have demonstrated that behavioral consultation has been effective in solving a variety of childhood problems (e.g., Gresham & Kendell, 1987; Martens, 1993). For example, this model has been demonstrated as effective with children exhibiting electively mute behavior (Piersel & Kratochwill, 1981; Sheridan, Kratochwill, & Ramirez, 1995), tics (Pray, Kramer, & Lindskog, 1986), social withdrawal (Sheridan, Kratochwill, & Elliott, 1990), academic and adjustment problems (Piersel & Kratochwill, 1979), and student underachievement (Galloway & Sheridan, 1994). The purposes of this chapter are to describe and define behavioral consultation, discuss its participants, and review the four basic stages of consultative problem solving. Readers are referred to the comprehensive texts by Bergan and Kratochwill (1990) and Kratochwill and Bergan (1990) for more extensive detail.

RATIONALE FOR CONSULTATION SERVICES

There are many reasons for considering consultation as a central activity for mental health service providers. First, several problems exist with the traditional direct "medical" model of service delivery. Such programs focus on an attempt to answer the question, "What is wrong with this child?" In other words, they center on assessing, diagnosing, and treating internal pathologies of children, rather than providing training and assistance to the environments in which children function (i.e., the environments that often contribute to or perpetuate the problems). We believe that services are most meaningful and effective when they directly address environmental variables related to the problems and when they work with significant adults who control those environments (Gutkin & Conoley, 1990).

A second reason for promoting consultation services concerns the ineffective and inefficient use of services commonly observed in educational and mental health settings. Traditional indirect assessment practices are very expensive, time-consuming, and unreliable. Furthermore, the functional utility of such approaches is limited (i.e., scores yield little information about instructional recommendations, base rates, or areas of competence). When direct intervention services are provided to children, they tend to be limited in terms of time, breadth, and depth. For example, individual or group treatments may be provided for 1 hour in a child's week, with little or no carryover to the settings in which the problem occurs.

A third rationale for consultation stems from the common problem of extensive caseloads. There continue to be daunting numbers of children and families in need of mental health and educational services. Natriello, McDill, and Pallas (1990) cited five key indicators associated with disadvantaged children and youth: (1) living in a poverty household, (2) being of a minority racial group, (3) living in a single-parent household, (4) having a poorly educated mother, and (5) having a non-English language background. They further estimate that at least 40% of children 17 years of age and younger experience any one (and often more) of these indicators, which may put them at risk for educational and social failure.

In 1989, 12% of all children below the age of 18 suffered from a mental disorder. Half of these cases were considered serious, yet fewer than one third were getting the help they needed. As many as 35% of kindergarten children currently go to school unprepared to learn. At present, 70% of mothers of school-age children are in the work force, as compared to 30% in 1960. Almost 50% of marriages end in divorce, and as of 1988, approximately 25% of children were living in single-parent families (the mother in 90% of the cases). Living in single-parent households is considered one of the major indicators for placing children at risk for educational failure (Educational Testing Service, 1992; Milne, Myers, Rosenthal, & Ginsburg, 1986). One third of marriages are remarriages, and one fourth of children have one or more stepparents (Braun & Swap, 1987).

Poverty and homelessness are additional problems facing families today. Almost one of four children live below the poverty line, and half the children living in single-parent homes are poor (Braun & Swap, 1987). The rate of poverty among families with young children almost doubled between 1973 and 1986 (Children's Defense Fund, 1989). The numbers rise with individuals from minority groups; in 1987, 45% of all African-American and 39% of Hispanic children were considered to be poor (Davis & McCaul, 1991). Further, young children in families represent the fastest growing single group of homeless in America today (Davis, 1991).

It is clear that several professional and client-related issues are facing service providers today. However, direct service models are insufficient in addressing complex and pervasive problems in a meaningful way (Gutkin & Conoley, 1990). According to Gutkin and Conoley (1990), "By providing treatment to children through primary caregivers such as parents and teachers, indirect services provide psychologists with a vehicle for influencing and modifying both the significant adults in children's lives and the children themselves" (p. 209).

CHARACTERISTICS OF BEHAVIORAL CONSULTATION

As traditionally conceived, behavioral consultation involves indirect services to a client (e.g., child) who is served through a consultee (e.g., parent, teacher) by a consultant (e.g., psychologist, special education teacher, social worker) (Bergan & Kratochwill, 1990; Kratochwill & Bergan, 1990). Specifically, behavioral consultation involves the problem-solving efforts of two or more persons to identify client needs and to develop, implement, and evaluate appropriate intervention strategies (Sheridan & Kratochwill, 1991). Although consultation typically is focused on solving "problems," consultation services can cover a wide spectrum of issues, including primary and secondary prevention and education. Several aspects of behavioral consultation make it a highly desirable practice in educational and mental health settings. First, it is a model of *indirect service delivery*, wherein a consultant works with a consultee who is responsible for providing direct services to a child-client. This approach may provide a broader and potentially more extensive effect on the consultee and client than other forms of direct service. When a professional works directly with a client in an individualized or small group format, services are provided to a small subset of students, and benefits may be limited to only those students who were the recipients of direct service. However, when consultation services are provided to a consultee, a larger number of clients can potentially receive services. This option is possible because in consultation, the *consultee* becomes the primary treatment agent. The consultee is thus empowered to use his or her skills and treatment strategies to resolve existing difficulties, address related issues, or prevent future problems in the natural environment.

A second benefit of behavioral consultation is its *problem-solving/decision-making orientation* for the treatment of academic, behavioral, and social difficulties. It is a goal-oriented model of service delivery that focuses on solutions to issues. Therefore, it is important that consultants not perceive their role as simply reactive (i.e., concerned only with solving presenting problems). Behavioral consultation should also be considered a proactive model used to facilitate the establishment of prevention programs or school-wide decisions. It should be noted also that the practice of behavioral consultation is not limited to dyads; rather, it can be implemented in small groups or work teams, although the latter approaches have not been featured often in the literature. Exceptions can be found in Rosenfield and Granois (in press) and Welch and Sheridan (1995), both of which present a model for extending behavioral consultation to apply to educational teams.

Behavioral consultation was devised within a tradition of *applied behavioral analysis* and technology (J. O. Cooper, Heron, & Heward, 1987; Kazdin, 1994). It is built upon a tradition of empirical, data-based research that can be translated into practice. The emphasis in behavioral consultation is on identifying an effective treatment for a consultee and client. Selection of a treatment may be based, in part, on a functional assessment aimed at establishing a functional relationship between environmental or task-specific variables and presenting problems, or on a treatment known to match a particular childhood problem or disorder. When important ecological factors can be identified, it may be possible to forge a direct link between effective interventions and assessment outcomes.

A third characteristic of behavioral consultation is that it implies a *collegial relationship* between the consultant and consultee. Although the consultant generally controls the verbal process of consultation, each of these individuals is considered to have special knowledge and/or expertise that is applied to facilitate problem resolution. For example, teachers are experts regarding important dimensions of the classroom setting. Their active involvement is essential to gain both broad and specific understandings of the instructional environment. It is important that the consultant's problem-solving expertise be joined with a consultee's situation-specific expertise to maximize consultation outcomes.

Finally, behavioral consultation involves a *structured interview process* consisting of problem identification, problem analysis, treatment (plan) implementation, and treatment (plan) evaluation. The interview sequence, complete with specific objectives and formal guides, aids consultants in structuring the problem-solving process. The structure is also highly desirable for research and training purposes.

PARTICIPANTS IN CONSULTATION

There are three primary roles in consultation; however, the individuals responsible for fulfilling these roles depend on specific situations. The consultation roles include consultant, consultee(s) and client(s).

The *consultant* is generally a psychologist, counselor, mental health worker, or special educator. The primary responsibility of the consultant is to understand the stages in the consultation process (i.e., problem identification, problem analysis, treatment [plan] implementation, and treatment [plan] evaluation) and guide consultees through these stages. Therefore, the consultant should have knowledge and skill in solving problems and making decisions (i.e., process expertise). The consultant also seeks out and helps to interpret important information about the child and assists in the selection of appropriate interventions. Thus, the consultant should also have knowledge and skill regarding the presenting problem and its treatment (i.e., content expertise). This is not to say that the consultant must be an "expert" in all areas, but she or he must have some substantive knowledge to promote problem solving. Finally, the consultant helps identify resources that are available to aid in problem resolution and monitors the implementation of interventions to ensure that beneficial services are provided to the client.

The *consultee* is the individual responsible for carrying out the intervention with the child-client. This person can be any individual who interacts with the client, such as a teacher, parent, paraprofessional, administrator, or extended family member. Traditionally, a single teacher or parent has been considered the consultee. The purpose of this text, however, is to suggest that individuals from various settings (such as home and school) serve as co-consultees. The practice of "conjoint behavioral consultation" joins parents, teachers, and other significant individuals from various systems. It promotes collaboration and consistency among home, school, and other programs with the active involvement of several consultees.

Consultees have specific roles in consultation. First, they must participate actively throughout the entire consultation process. In a structured behavioral consultation format, consultees are asked to describe specific problems by sharing their observations of the client. They are also responsible for working directly with the client (i.e., implementing the treatment program) and should work with the consultant to develop a program that is manageable, feasible, and acceptable. When parents and teachers are involved as co-consultees, they share the responsibility of communicating with each other and building a home–school relationship that will allow them to carry out programs in the future.

In behavioral consultation, the *client* is generally a student experiencing behavioral, social, or academic difficulties. In some cases, there may be a group of clients, such as a classroom of students. The client's primary role is to participate in the treatment program and to change in the direction of the consultation goals. Depending on various client-related factors (e.g., age, level of intellectual functioning, severity of problems), the client may participate to some extent in establishing the goals of consultation and in designing and implementing plans for behavior change. Although the client's active participation may blur the distinction between direct and indirect service, it may increase feelings of ownership and involvement of some clients. This involvement may be particularly important for older or potentially resistant clients (such as adolescents).

Recent advances in behavioral consultation suggest that the client in consultation can vary (Bergan & Kratochwill, 1990; Kratochwill & Bergan, 1990). For example, the client may be an individual student, a classroom teacher, or an entire organization. In these cases, the level at which problems are defined and analyzed will change, and the manner in which the client role is enacted will vary. For example, when an entire school body is the client, treatment targets may include increasing staff participation in meetings or involving parents as volunteers. The conditions surrounding these broad areas (e.g., contingencies operating in staff meetings or parent demographics) are likely to be complex and multifaceted.

STAGES OF BEHAVIORAL CONSULTATION

Behavioral consultation is typically described as occurring in four general stages (i.e., problem identification, problem analysis, treatment [plan] implementation, and treatment [plan] evaluation). The stages are described linearly, but often overlap in practice. Procedurally, they are operationalized through a series of standardized interviews. The objectives of each stage are stated in Table 1.1, which also provides sample interview questions. In *problem identification,* the consultant and consultee specify and define the problem or problems to be targeted in consultation. In *problem analysis,* they explore the problem by evaluating baseline data and identifying the variables that might facilitate problem solution. On the basis of this analysis, a plan is designed to solve the target problem. During the *treatment (plan) implementation* stage, the behavioral intervention that was designed during problem analysis is put into operation. Finally, the *treatment (plan) evaluation* stage is undertaken to determine the effectiveness of the plan and discuss procedures for maintenance and generalization.

Problem Identification

Early behavioral consultation research has suggested that the best predictor for effective consultation outcomes is a clear definition of the problem (Bergan & Tombari, 1976). Therefore, the most important stage of consultation may be problem identification. This stage requires specific and precise clarification of the problem to be addressed. If problems are defined incompletely or incorrectly, problem solving will likely be ineffective or terminated prematurely. Therefore, adequate time and effort must be devoted to problem-identification efforts.

The *problem identification* stage of behavioral consultation goes beyond defining the problem or problems that will be the target of consultation. During this stage, the consultant and consultees also designate the goal or goals to be achieved through consultation, assess current client performance, and determine the extent of the problem by identifying the discrepancy between current and desired client performance.

Table 1.1. Objectives and Sample Questions of Behavioral Consultation Stages

Problem Identification Interview (PII)

Objectives
   Define the problem(s) in behavioral terms.
   Identify important environmental conditions that impact the behavior.
   Provide a tentative strength of the behavior.
   Discuss and reach agreement on a goal for behavior change.
   Establish a procedure for collection of baseline data.
Sample Interview Questions
   Give me some examples of your concerns. Which of these behaviors is most problematic?
   Where does the child display this behavior? Give me some examples of where this occurs.
      Which of the settings is most problematic?
   What typically happens before the behavior occurs?
   What else is typically happening in the classroom/playground/home when the behavior
      occurs?
   What typically happens after the behavior occurs?
   How often does this behavior occur? How long does it last?
   What would be an acceptable level of this behavior?
   What would be a simple way for you to keep track of the behavior?

Problem Analysis Interview (PAI)

Objectives
   Evaluate and obtain agreement on the baseline data.
   Conduct an ecological analysis of the behavior.
   Design an intervention plan including specification of conditions to be changed and the
      practical guidelines regarding treatment implementation.
   Reaffirm record-keeping procedures.
Sample Interview Questions
   Were you able to keep a record of the behavior?
   According to the data, Paul completed 50% of his work on Monday, Wednesday, and
      Thursday. Is that right?
   What did you notice before the problem occurred? What things may have led up to its
      occurrence?
   What typically happened after the occurrence of the behavior? What types of things did you
      notice afterward?
   What else was happening in the classroom/playground/home when the behavior occurred?
      What time of day or day of week seemed most problematic? What patterns did you
      notice?
   What can be done to reach our goal?
   Can we continue the same recording procedure as before?

Treatment (Plan) Implementation

Objectives
   Monitor implementation of the intervention.

Table 1.1. (Continued)

Provide training to treatment agent, if necessary.
Determine need for immediate revisions in plan.
Continue data collection procedures.

Treatment (Plan) Evaluation Interview (TEI)

Objectives
Evaluate treatment data and determine whether the goals of consultation have been met.
Evaluate the effectiveness of the treatment plan.
Discuss strategies and tactics regarding the continuation, modification, or termination of the
   treatment plan.
Discuss strategies for maintenance and generalization of treatment gains.
Sample Interview Questions
How did things go with the plan?
Has the goal been met?
Do you think that the behavior program was responsible for the change in Stan's behavior?
Do you think this plan would work with another child with similar difficulties?)
Should we leave the plan in effect for a while longer?
How could we encourage Jennifer to display these behavior changes in other settings? What
   procedures should we use to make sure that she continues to show positive behavior
   change over time?
How can we modify the procedures so that the plan is more effective?
How can we monitor the child's progress to ensure that these positive changes continue?

Source: Adapted from Welch, M., & Sheridan, S. M. (1995). *Educational partnerships: Serving students at risk*. San Antonio, TX: Harcourt Brace. Reproduced with permission.

Considerations in Problem Identification

Most if not all problems brought to a consultant will be complex. It is important to clarify the various parts or components of a problem and then to identify a place to begin (i.e., a priority). This sequence makes problem resolution more manageable and probable. For example, an aggressive adolescent ("Kevin") may be described by his teacher as verbally and physically assaultive, oppositional, and impulsive. He may fail to complete his work and be considered at risk for academic failure. He may provoke other students and be rejected by them at school. Clearly, all of these problems are important. However, to try to solve them all at once would be overwhelming. In problem identification, one of these behaviors (e.g., physical assaultiveness or lack of work completion) might be selected as a target behavior.

There are a number of considerations to keep in mind when selecting the target of consultation (for a review of some important issues, see Kratochwill, 1985). Often, behaviors that are physically dangerous to the client or others are selected first. Alternatively, behaviors that are aversive to others because of their deviance or unpredictability are often targeted. It is helpful to select a behavior that will maximize the client's flexibility and promote long-term individual or social good. In some situations, behaviors can be identified that serve as antecedents to other inappropriate behaviors and, if controlled, can have positive effects on other collateral behaviors. For example, it might be noted that a child who is failing math is frequently late to class, fails to have work materials ready, and fails to turn in assignments. Treating tardiness may have positive effects on his readiness and work-completion behaviors.

It is also important to select for changing those behaviors that the environment will continue to maintain. For example, appropriate social skills, promptness, and work completion and accuracy are all behaviors that will likely be reinforced naturally even when treatment contingencies are withdrawn.

Once the target problem is identified, it is important to develop a clear definition. *Operational definitions* specify problems or behaviors in terms that are observable, concrete, specific, and objective. These criteria are important to ensure that all participants (consultants, parents, and teachers) clearly understand the problem to be addressed. Also, because teachers and parents will be requested to collect data on the target behavior, it is essential that they all operate with the same definition in mind. In the example of Kevin, "physical aggression" might be defined as "use of physical force (i.e., kicking, hitting, striking out at peers) when engaged in group activities on the playground."

When specifying a problem to target in consultation, it is important to define the problem in such a way that something can be done about it. This focus emphasizes the importance of identifying environmental events that can be targeted and altered, rather than discussing internal conditions that are largely outside the realm of educational interventions. For example, some consultees may try to define a problem student as having a learning disability, an alcoholic parent, or a brain injury. Although these conditions may be established, focusing solely on the educational label, the family dysfunction, or the internal medical problem allows little control over remediation. In other words, consultants and consultees can do little to "fix" a problem when it is defined in these terms. Alternatively, a problem can be defined in terms of its manifestations (e.g., "Kevin engages in negative physical contact [kicking, hitting, striking out] with peers 5 times per week") or in terms of environmental conditions (e.g., "Kevin engages in negative physical contact [i.e., kicking, hitting, striking out] with peers when engaged in group activities on the playground"). In this way, consultants and consultees will have more control over the treatment and resolution of the problem.

To ensure that the expectations of consultation are clear and appropriate, it is helpful to define both the current and the desired situation. This tactic allows all individuals involved in consultation to understand the goals for problem solving and can be accomplished by determining desired and acceptable outcomes. *Goal specification* provides clear and objective direction to the process. Likewise, it provides consultants and consultees a means for measuring attainment of consultation objectives.

It is often helpful to state the behavior to be changed in positive terms. In other words, it is important to specify what the client *should* do, not just what he or she should refrain from doing. For example, a goal for a physically aggressive child might be stated as "Kevin will initiate and maintain positive interactions with other students," rather than as "Kevin will not hit others."

In data-based decision making, the collection of baseline data will be required to determine the actual severity of a problem and environmental factors affecting its occurrence. After the target problem is identified, a method for data collection should be developed. In general, consultees will be responsible for collecting behavioral information on a regular basis. Therefore, it is imperative that they assist in developing procedures for data collection and find the methods simple and practical. For example, a simple tally method documenting frequency of a behavior at predetermined points in time is more desirable than methods requiring the consultee to monitor several behavioral or environmental conditions simultaneously. Although the latter may be important to understand the function of a problem behavior, an additional observer (e.g., the consultant) may be necessary to collect such extensive behavioral data. Nevertheless, this data-based approach to problem solving is important in analyzing the problem accurately, designing an intervention based on the data, and evaluating the effectiveness of consultation.

Problem Identification Interview

The problem identification process is initiated by means of a Problem Identification Interview (PII). The major objectives for this interview and sample interview questions are presented in Table 1.1.

Problem Analysis

The *problem analysis* stage of behavioral consultation is conducted when data collected during problem identification indicate the existence of a problem in need of attention. Problem analysis occurs in two broad phases. The first is the *analysis phase,* during which the consultant and consultees analyze the environmental factors or events that appear to be contributing to the problem. These same factors could be used in a plan to promote problem solution. The *plan design phase* involves the development of plans to remediate the problem.

Analysis Phase

One way to examine environmental events is by conducting *conditions or functional analyses,* that is, exploring antecedent, consequent, and sequential conditions. *Antecedent conditions* are events that precede the occurrence of a problematic situation. For example, in the case of Kevin, his teacher may be asked to identify events that typically happen before the lunch recess or those that precede the aggressive outbursts. The teacher may be able to identify common occurrences, such as Kevin's failing to get selected on a team or being teased by peers. *Consequent conditions* are environmental events that follow the problem. In response to a question about what generally happens after Kevin engages in physically aggressive acts, his teacher may recall that he typically returns to the school building and waits up to one hour for the principal to talk to him. On some occasions, he is sent home. This information is important, because these environmental conditions (e.g., antecedents and consequences) can be altered in an intervention designed to decrease Kevin's physical aggression and increase his appropriate social behaviors. *Sequential conditions* are common patterns across problematic occasions, such as time of day or day of week. For example, Kevin's teacher may recognize that his rate of aggression is highest on days when groups of students convene on the playground without structured games (e.g., soccer). His aggression may be generally worse on Mondays and Wednesdays, when science class is scheduled after recess and when his mother is at home. There may be no formal rules for student behavior on the playground, and recess monitors might avoid the area where 6th-grade boys congregate.

Exploring events in this way may clarify some practical and effective methods of altering the environment to decrease Kevin's aggressive behaviors and increase his prosocial skills. For example, antecedent conditions can be modified by ensuring that formal games or activities are planned during lunch recess. Consequent conditions can be altered by instituting a remedial program geared toward teaching Kevin effective conflict management skills, rather than sending him home or to the principal. Sequential conditions can be manipulated by changing the science instruction time to the morning hours and not letting Kevin know the days on which his mother will be at home.

Table 1.2. Conducting Skills Analyses

1. Identify the target skill that should be present.
2. Break the skill down into its component parts.
3. Assess the target student's ability to perform each component subskill.
4. Determine the uppermost level at which the target student can perform to mastery.
5. Develop an intervention for the student, starting at the point at which he or she demonstrates mastery.

Conditions analyses are important to explore when the target problem is behavioral in nature (e.g., inattention, fighting, skipping school). However, in some situations it will be important to conduct a *skills analysis* along with or in place of a conditions analysis. Skills analyses allow consultants and consultees to explore the skill level of an individual or group of individuals when the concern is one of ability. For example, skills analyses are appropriate to determine the level of a student's academic or social skills. The steps of a skills analysis are presented in Table 1.2.

Taking the example of Kevin, it may be questioned during problem analysis whether he has adequate social skills to initiate prosocial interactions or engage in cooperative play. A statement on the part of the teacher or parent is usually inadequate to make this determination. For example, observing Kevin on the playground over a period of 4 or 5 days may reveal that his typical style at joining ongoing group games is to approach peers, grab the game ball, and announce that he will participate. If he virtually never demonstrates an appropriate entry into the game, it is likely that he does not know how; that is, he does not have that skill within his repertoire. The demonstration of a *skill deficit* suggests that it is necessary to include instruction and practice with feedback in an intervention. On the other hand, these same observations may reveal that on some days Kevin uses the inappropriate approach suggested above, but on other days he demonstrates patience and self-control by waiting for a break in the game and asking one team leader if he can join. It can be assumed, then, that Kevin has the ability to use appropriate entry behaviors but does not do so consistently. These circumstances suggest a *performance deficit* and indicate that operant techniques designed to reinforce and maintain appropriate behaviors could be included in the treatment.

Plan Design Phase

The plan design phase of problem analysis follows directly from the analysis phase. On the basis of observations of consultees and the data collected, it is often possible to speculate about the purpose of problem behaviors. In other words, it may be possible to formulate hypotheses about why a student demonstrates noncompliant or aggressive behaviors. If behavioral observations suggest environmental factors that may be supporting or reinforcing problems, consultants and consultees can develop interventions to change these environmental conditions and, hence, address the problem. Therefore, it is important for consultants to inquire about what may be maintaining or reinforcing the problem behavior. Even after extended observations and data collection, consultees may not have ideas about environmental events or variables. If they continue to state internal or psychological reasons (e.g., "Kevin acts that way because he is hyperactive"), their attributions should be restated in environmental or skill-based terms (e.g., "Kevin may hit peers on the playground because he is then allowed to go into the school and wait for the principal, which generally excuses him from science class" or "Kevin may hit peers on the playground because he does not have the skills to initiate structured play activities appropriately"). This information will set the stage for developing a plan that addresses these issues directly.

Problem Analysis Interview

Problem analysis is implemented through a Problem Analysis Interview (PAI). In this interview, the consultant and consultees decide on the existence of a problem that warrants attention. Conditions and/or skills are discussed that might influence the child's behavior. A plan is then designed by the consultant and consultee(s) to attempt problem solution. Table 1.1 outlines the objectives of problem analysis, with sample interview questions.

Treatment (Plan) Implementation

The third stage in behavioral consultation is *treatment (plan) implementation*. During this stage, the plan designed in problem analysis is put into operation. The objective of consultation during treatment implementation is to maximize the likelihood that the plan will produce desired outcomes. Although there is no formal interview during treatment implementation, there are several types of interactions that may occur between the consultant and consultee(s). For example, brief contacts with consultees are important to monitor implementation of the plan. Observations of consultee and student behaviors are important to monitor consultees' treatment implementation skills and clients' responsiveness to the intervention. In some cases, revisions will be necessary, and a brief contact and observations will be useful in pointing out this necessity. In some cases, training sessions will also be necessary if observations suggest that consultees do not have the knowledge or skills to implement the plan with integrity. Table 1.1 presents the major objectives of this stage.

The acceptability of treatments should also be considered during treatment implementation. *Treatment acceptability* is defined as "judgments by lay persons, clients, and others of whether treatment procedures are appropriate, fair, and reasonable for the problem client" (Kazdin, 1981, p. 493). If consultees find a treatment unacceptable in terms of their time, resources, or other practical and theoretical aspects, it is likely that the treatment will not be implemented or will be implemented incorrectly (Witt, Martens, & Elliott, 1984). The theoretical orientation of the consultee, the time and/or resources required to implement the intervention, and any perceived lack of effectiveness of the plan are variables that might contribute to the degree to which a consultee finds a treatment desirable (Witt et al., 1984). In consultation, then, consultants and consultees work together to develop a plan that is acceptable in terms of criteria that are both objective (i.e., based on sound empirical support) and subjective (i.e., acceptable to the consultees) (Gutkin & Curtis, 1990).

Treatment (Plan) Evaluation

After a treatment has been in effect for a period of time (usually a week or longer), the *treatment (plan) evaluation* stage of behavioral consultation is undertaken to determine whether the goals of consultation have been attained and whether the plan has been effective at producing behavioral change in the client. Depending on the client's responsiveness to treatment, treatment evaluation may indicate that consultation and the intervention should be continued, terminated, or modified. If modifications are made in the original plan, the consultation process recycles through the treatment implementation and evaluation stages. In some cases, the goals will have been met and procedures for generalizing the behavior change to nontreatment settings or behaviors can be undertaken. In complex cases, a reassessment of problematic behaviors not initially addressed in consultation occurs. An effective means for reassessment is to recycle through the entire four-stage model to identify, analyze, and treat new target behaviors. Once all goals are met, procedures for maintenance and generalization should be discussed.

Treatment Evaluation Interview

Treatment evaluation is initiated through the Treatment Evaluation Interview (TEI). In this interview, the consultant and consultee(s) determine whether goal attainment has been achieved. The need for further problem identification or analysis is discussed and, when appropriate, plans are established to reduce the likelihood of problem recurrence. Table 1.1 reviews the objectives of treatment evaluation and presents sample interview questions.

RESEARCH IN BEHAVIORAL CONSULTATION

Reviews of the empirical literature have suggested that consultation is an effective model of educational service delivery (Mannino & Shore, 1975; Medway, 1979; Medway & Updyke, 1985). Among the various models of consultation, the behavioral approach has received considerable research attention (Alpert & Yammer, 1983) and some empirical support (Medway & Updyke, 1985). Research on consultation has focused on both outcome and process variables (Gresham & Kendell, 1987).

Outcome Research

Several recent experimental studies have illustrated the effectiveness of behavioral consultation in effecting client change (e.g., Fuchs & Fuchs, 1989; Fuchs, Fuchs, & Bahr, 1990; Pray et al., 1986; Sheridan, 1992; Sheridan et al., 1990; for a review, see Bergan & Kratochwill, 1990). For example, underachieving students whose parents and teachers received consultation services during elementary school demonstrated more significant gains in several academic areas upon graduation from high school than did a control group (Jackson, Cleveland, & Merenda, 1975). Fuchs et al. (1990) demonstrated the effectiveness of behavioral consultation in decreasing referrals for testing and improving teachers' perceptions of difficult-to-teach students. Pray et al. (1986) reported a comprehensive case study in which the tic behaviors of an elementary-age student were decreased upon the implementation of a behavioral consultation intervention.

Along with benefits to clients, change in the consultee has been demonstrated as an outcome of behavioral consultation. T. K. Anderson, Kratchwill, and Bergan (1986) documented the effectiveness of an experimental training package for increasing teachers' knowledge of behavioral procedures and for increasing the frequency of teacher verbalizations regarding overt child behaviors and behavioral intervention plans during the first two stages of behavioral consultation. In addition, these researchers demonstrated that specific rather than general consultant questions were important in eliciting consultee statements related to environmental conditions surrounding behavior. Behavioral consultation has also been found to lead to higher teacher expectations regarding their ability to solve problems and to teach a child with academic difficulties. This outcome, in turn, leads to greater utilization of effective instructional strategies (Bergan, Byrnes, & Kratochwill, 1979; Tombari & Bergan, 1978).

In another study investigating outcomes of behavioral consultation involving teacher consultees, Tunnecliffe, Leach, and Tunnecliffe (1986) compared the effectiveness of two teacher stress management techniques (i.e., "collaborative behavioral consultation" and relaxation training) in reducing stress in teachers. These researchers found greater maintenance of treatment effects in the consultation condition as compared to a control group. Similar ongoing effects were not found for the relaxation training group.

Process Research

Along with enhancing educational and professional outcomes, some research has examined the process of behavioral consultation. Early research by Bergan and Tombari (1975, 1976) demonstrated that the most important process variable in consultation is problem identification. The manner in which questions are asked is important. Consultant questions that use behavioral cues and elicit specific information about environmental conditions surrounding behaviors are particularly effective (T. K. Anderson et al., 1986; Tombari & Bergan, 1978). Teachers are most likely to identify methods and resources for carrying out a consultation plan if consultants ask them, rather than tell them, how they can identify and use resources (Bergan & Neumann, 1980).

Erchul and his colleagues (Erchul, 1987; Erchul & Chewning, 1990; Erchul, Hughes, Meyers, Hickman, & Braden, 1992) examined interactional processes in consultation. Consistent with the importance placed on consultant questioning skills (Tombari & Bergan, 1978), they have found that consultants tend to control behavioral consultation interactions. In fact, the frequency of consultant requests is positively related to consultant effectiveness, and the frequency of consultee requests is negatively related to consultant effectiveness. Likewise, the more the consultant and consultee agree on their respective roles and the process and goals of consultation, the more positive are consultees' evaluations of consultation outcomes and the consultant's effectiveness. The general findings of this line of research have indicated that effective consultation can be characterized by the concepts of cooperation and teamwork, where roles are clear and active participation by all parties is valued.

Although behavioral consultation is considered effective, research traditionally has been focused on a narrow range of ecological settings (i.e., schools and classrooms) with a narrow scope (i.e., teachers as consultees) (Kratochwill, Sheridan, & Van Someren, 1988). It is beneficial to implement consultation procedures with individuals beyond the school setting only. In particular, the home setting, and the interactions and relationships between parents and teachers are vital to a child's social, behavioral, and academic success (Becher, 1986). Unfortunately, parental involvement in educational problem solving remains low. Despite the good intentions of teachers, parents, and mental health professionals, the most effective way to operationalize collaborative home–school partnerships is unclear. In this text, behavioral consultation is presented as a practical model that provides a structure for professionals to work effectively with parents and teachers together.

DISCUSSION QUESTIONS

1	Describe the four-stage behavioral consultation model. How is this model the same as and different from other models of service delivery (e.g., direct service)?
2	What are some of the general and specific benefits of behavioral consultation?
3	What might be some difficulties with conducting behavioral consultation?
4	Under what conditions would behavioral consultation be particularly useful? When might behavioral consultation be contraindicated?
5	What are some specific research ideas in the area of behavioral consultation? How might one go about investigating such issues?

2

Models for Working with Parents

Upon completing this chapter, readers should be able to:

1. Distinguish between parent education, parent training, and parent consultation in terms of their goals and procedures.
2. Report the major research findings associated with the various models of working with parents.
3. Define parent involvement and home–school collaboration.
4. Articulate various benefits of parent involvement in education.
5. Discuss the importance of effective communication with parents.
6. Define the open communication skills of clarification, attending, paraphrasing, and summarizing.

INTRODUCTION

In recent decades, the challenges facing families have become tremendously complex. Problems such as divorce, poverty, child abuse, teenage pregnancy, and juvenile crime are becoming more prevalent in society. Mental health professionals are recognizing the need to work with parents and families to maximize treatment outcomes for children. The purposes of this chapter are to review briefly some of the common approaches to working with parents and provide practical recommendations for doing so.

Several alternatives to working with parents are available. In general, three models are typically suggested: parent education, parent training, and parent consultation. In educational settings, these are often subsumed under a broader umbrella of "parent involvement." Although the aforementioned three terms are often used interchangeably, there are some important differences. Sheridan (1993) described differences between parent education, training, and consultation across a number of dimensions (i.e., breadth of

	Dimensions			
	Breadth of information disseminated	Depth of skill development	Specificity of skill and knowledge imparted	Individuality of focus
Parent education	High	Low	Low	Low
Parent training	Medium	Medium	Medium	Medium
Parent consultation	Low	High	High	High

Figure 2.1. Matrix characterizing various models for working with parents across dimensions of breadth, depth, specificity, and individuality. (*Source*: Sheridan, S. M. [1993]. Parent consultation: Current trends and future directions. In J. E. Zins, T. R. Kratochwill, & S. N. Elliott [Eds.], *The handbook of consultation services for children: Applications in educational and clinical settings* [p. 111]. San Francisco: Jossey-Bass. Reproduced with permission.)

information disseminated, depth of skill development, specificity of skill and knowledge imparted, and individuality of focus). A matrix characterizing these service-delivery models across each dimension is presented in Figure 2.1.

Although differences between models are apparent, there are some unifying characteristics. All models have one or more children as clients, and services are provided through the parents. Thus, parent education and parent training often can be included in a parent consultation approach. Examples in which parent training occurs within the context of a consultative relationship can be found in Carrington Rotto and Kratochwill (1994) and Taverne and Sheridan (1995).

PARENT EDUCATION AND TRAINING

Parent Education

Parent education has been defined as "a systematic and conceptually based program, intended to impart information, awareness, or skills to the participants on aspects of parenting" (Fine, 1980, pp. 5–6). Models of parent education are generally concerned with educating parents about child development, communication, or other aspects of family life. In general, parent education programs do not explore the manner in which parenting, family dynamics, and home conditions relate to a child's learning and behavior at school. They typically depend on lectures and discussions to disseminate information and change parents' attitudes (Kramer, 1990a). The goals of parent education include helping parents achieve greater self-awareness, improve parent–child communication, make family life more enjoyable, and aquire useful information on child development (Fine, 1980).

In most parent education programs, limited attention is given to parents' personal problems. Some discussion of interpersonal communication is typical; however, programs do not generally instruct parents on changing interactional styles with their children. The focus is typically on achieving changes in a predetermined number and length of sessions without effecting intensive personality or behavioral changes in parents (Dembo, Sweitzer, & Lauritzen, 1985). Fine (1980, 1989) provides comprehensive discussions of parent education programs for interested readers.

Parent Training

According to Dembo et al. (1985), "*parent training*, which is subsumed under parent education, is defined as a process that includes at least one component, teaching specific skills" (p. 156; italics added). Some parent training models are broad programs that attempt to train general parenting skills, such as effective discipline or compliance training. Others are designed to remediate specific behavioral problems such as social skills (Sheridan & Dee, in preparation) or to develop discrete skills at behavioral management (such as the use of positive reinforcement or timeout) (Jenson, Rhode, & Reavis, in press). Several sources are available to readers interested in learning more about parent training (e.g., Dangel & Polster, 1984, 1988; Dembo et al., 1985; Fine, 1980, 1989; Kramer, 1990b; Sanders & Dadds, 1993).

Three general theoretical approaches have received the most attention in the parent training literature: humanistic, Adlerian, and behavioral (Dembo et al., 1985). *Humanistic approaches* focus on teaching parents relationship-building strategies such as the use of active listening, sending "I-messages," and negotiation between parent and child. An example of humanistic programs is Parent Effectiveness Training (PET) (Gordon, 1975). *Adlerian approaches* attempt to help parents understand their children, their thought processes, and what motivates their behaviors. The assumption in these programs is that by understanding childrens' motives and actions, parents will be in a better position to use effective strategies. An example of an Adlerian program is Systematic Training for Effective Parenting (STEP) (Dinkmeyer & McKay, 1976). *Behavioral programs* are quite diverse and typically review basic behavioral concepts, provide information regarding the manner in which child behaviors shape parent responses, and attempt to teach parents skills with which to shift contingencies for children's behaviors. These programs are based on the assumption that behavior is learned and sustained by the positive and negative reinforcement children receive from social agents, especially parents. Specific training in the nature and use of reinforcers, observations and recording procedures, and techniques for eliminating undesirable and strengthening desirable responses are highlighted (Dembo et al., 1985; Dumas, 1989).

Several effective behavioral parent training programs have been developed, such as those described by Barkley (1987, 1990), Forehand and McMahon (1981), Patterson, Reid, Jones, and Conger (1975), Sanders and Dadds (1993), and Webster-Stratton (1987). They all share common features that emphasize the acquisition and performance of specific behavioral management skills. Parent trainers typically use methods such as discussion, modeling, role-playing, guided practice, and homework assignments (Dumas, 1989; Kramer, 1990a,b). Written materials and videotaped examples are sometimes incorporated into training (e.g., Webster-Stratton, 1987, 1990; Webster-Stratton, Hollinsworth, & Kolpacoff, 1989).

Behavioral parent training programs have been implemented in both individual and group formats. In *individual parent training*, the consultant focuses on an individual set of parents and provides not only direct training, but also direct supervision of the parents as the treatment program is developed and implemented. The goals of the individual format are to change the parents' behaviors while remediating their children's problematic behavior and to teach parents child-rearing skills to generalize to future situations. Examples can be found in Forehand and McMahon (1981), Carrington Rotto and Kratochwill (1994), and Taverne and Sheridan (1995).

In the *group parent training* approach, groups of parents are given instruction in behavioral child-management skills. All techniques include supervised practice in either analogue or in vivo situations. Improvement in the change agents' child-management skills and in the target child's behaviors are among the major foci of these programs. Patterson and his associates (e.g., Patterson & Reid, 1973; Patterson et al., 1975) have developed a comprehensive program illustrating the group training format, based heavily on social learning theory.

Research Findings and Limitations

Parent education and training have been effective at resolving child behavior problems, altering parental attitudes, and enhancing parent–child relationships (Dembo et al., 1985; Dumas, 1989). Given the different assumptions, goals, and objectives of humanistic, Adlerian, and behavioral approaches, comparative outcome studies are difficult to conduct. For example, humanistic and Adlerian programs typically assess parental child-rearing attitudes as the primary outcome measure. The PET program (Gordon, 1975) has yielded mixed results in this area. Some Adlerian approaches have indicated positive changes in child-rearing attitudes (Dinkmeyer & McKay, 1976). However, additional research revealed that following involvement in an Adlerian-based program (Active Parenting) (Popkin, 1983), parents did not improve their knowledge of behavioral principles of child management. Likewise, there is little evidence that such programs produce change in the targeted child's behavior (Dembo et al., 1985). Parental reports of child behavior and child self-concept also remained unchanged (Kramer, 1990b; Weise, 1989). It is therefore difficult to draw conclusions regarding differential effectiveness of the various approaches.

Behavioral parent training programs have received the greatest focus of research attention and generally have yielded promising results. In a meta-analysis of the parent education and training literature, Medway (1989) concluded that the behavioral model had the greatest effects on child behavior measures. Furthermore, Dembo and his colleagues suggest that behavioral parent training studies have fewer methodological flaws and utilize a larger number of outcome variables.

Although parent education and training programs typically report positive outcomes in relation to their stated goals, many investigations have contained methodological problems. Limitations have been found in such areas as outcome evaluations, reliability of observations, clinical utility, and cost-effectiveness. Few studies provide information on consultation and treatment integrity, leader characteristics, and acceptability of the procedures. Assessment of generalization and maintenance of treatment effects, family variables that may affect treatment outcome, and contiguous covariation in parents' and children's behaviors are not typically examined (Bijou, 1984; Dembo et al., 1985; Kramer, 1990b; Medway, 1989; Moreland, Schwebel, Beck, & Wells, 1982). Further, there is typically only scant information provided in regard to operational procedures (Dembo et al., 1985). Although most studies report the general model espoused, the consistency with which procedures are applied is typically left unreported (Medway, 1989).

PARENT CONSULTATION

Overview of Models

Similar to the distinctions within parent training, Cobb and Medway (1978) suggested three theoretical approaches to parent consultation (i.e., reflective, child guidance, and behavioral). Reflective parent consultation models emphasize parental awareness, understanding, and acceptance of a child's feelings based on the assumption that this tactic may influence the child's behaviors and the interpersonal relationship between parent and child. In many respects, this approach is similar to the Adlerian parent training approaches. Child guidance consultation approaches are concerned with the clinical diagnosis and interpretation of a child's problems in analytical or intrapsychic terms. The result of consultation in these cases is typically referral for psychiatric treatment. Behavioral parent consultation emphasizes actual observable behavior and the environmental conditions that strengthen, reinforce, and maintain inappropriate behavior patterns.

In an early conceptualization of "family consultation," Bergan and Duley (1981) described an extension of behavioral consultation that considered the family system as the client. Incorporating a family systems perspective, they described difficulties in family functioning as central to behavioral manifestations in the "dysfunctional member." Consistent with a family systems or social learning perspective, these authors describe behaviors of each family member as reciprocally influencing each other member. According to this model, three types of messages can be communicated by the consultee (i.e., factual, inferential, and affective). Consistent with the behavioral consultation tradition, methods of guiding the consultee's communication through the use of emitters and elicitors were also suggested.

Although the recognition of the family-as-system represents an important extension of behavioral consultation, at least two limitations of traditional behavioral consultation can be identified. First, although interactions within the family system are recognized, the interactions between the home and school systems are not addressed. Second, Bergan and Duley imply that the source of "pathology" resides within the child. Assessment is thus limited to child behavior, and interventions are directed primarily at changing only the child's inappropriate behavior. It is likely that a child's difficulty is often the result of several environmental, situational, and interactional factors that permeate beyond the home or school in isolation. A model of consultation that acknowledges the relationship between the home and school and that broadens the scope of assessment and intervention to address variables at this level would be beneficial. Conjoint behavioral consultation, as described in the remainder of this text, is concerned with these important conceptual and practical dimensions.

Work in the area of brief psychotherapy has provided the basis for a new model of family consultation. Carlson, Hickman, and Horton (1992) described a model of "solution-oriented family–school consultation adapted

from the brief psychotherapy models for working with individuals and families" (p. 197). The focus of the model is on solution identification, with the
consultant working with the client, the client's teachers, and the family.
Attention is paid to identifying strengths for resolving difficulties, and exceptions to the problem. The phases of their consultation model include introduction, explaining the solution-oriented approach, joining, negotiating a
solvable complaint, establishing a solution goal, agreeing on the smallest
change, eliciting multiple solutions to accomplish the smallest change, clarifying individual responsibilities, follow-up, and evaluating and recycling if
necessary.

Brown, Pryzwansky, and Schulte (1995) presented an eclectic model of
family consultation, guided by general assumptions from social learning,
mental health, and systems theories. Their stages of family consultation,
which are similar to those of behavioral consultation, include structuring and
relationship building, assessment/problem identification, goal setting, explaining psychological principles, selecting intervention strategies, and
evaluation/follow-up. Important components of this model include the recognition of relationship variables and the delineation of specific and pragmatic
recommendations to assist consultants in strengthening interpersonal relations with parents.

Parent Consultation Research

Few systematic studies of behavioral parent consultation have been
conducted. Bergan, Reddy, Feld, Sladaczek, and Schwarz (1991) examined
the effects of behavioral parent consultation on kindergarten children's summer learning of math and reading skills. Consultation services were examined
in relation to the effects of school socioeconomic status (SES) on learning.
Volunteer families were assigned at random to consultation treatment and
control conditions. Treatment parents received consultation assistance to
provide summer learning opportunities for their children. Structural equation
modeling revealed a direct effect of school SES on learning during the school
year and an indirect effect on learning over the summer. Parent consultation
provided at the beginning of the summer directly influenced summer learning.
Three important variations of behavioral consultation practice that the researchers used are worth noting: (1) problem identification and problem
analysis interviews were conducted together; (2) all interviews were carried
out over the telephone, with no face-to-face contact with consultees; and (3)
consultant verbal behaviors were not systematically evaluated.

Recently, Carrington Rotto and Kratochwill (1994) reported the results of a parent consultation study that integrated competency-based parent training with behavioral consultation. Parents participated in a competency-based instructional format in which they learned differential attention, instruction-giving, and time-out skills to mastery. Parents were then involved in implementing the treatment for their elementary-age children (N = 4) who exhibited clinical levels of noncompliance at home. The results of the study demonstrated that the parents acquired the skills and decreased the children's noncompliance in the home setting.

In general, many of the parent consultation investigations are plagued with methodological flaws. An early review of the parent consultation literature concluded that many researchers fail to control for the effects of individual consultants, do not describe experimental procedures sufficiently to allow for cross-study comparisons, and do not use broad dependent variables (both immediately and at follow-up) that tap a wide range of parent and child behaviors (Cobb & Medway, 1978).

An additional weakness in the parent consultation literature concerns the limited information typically provided in regard to specific operational procedures used to implement consultation. Although several reports indicate that "parent consultation" occurred (e.g., Humes & Clark, 1989; Palmo & Kuzinar, 1972; Strother & Jacobs, 1986; Wright, 1976), the specific procedures used typically are unidentified. Furthermore, definitional inconsistencies are apparent, as much of this work involves simply a combination of parent training and direct child intervention.

PARENT INVOLVEMENT

Compared to parent education, training, and consultation, service-delivery models that emphasize home-school relationships are receiving increased attention in the professional literature (for an overview, see Plunge, Waters-Guetschow, Kratochwill, & Gettinger, 1995). The importance of working with families in educational settings is supported by a plethora of empirical studies attesting to its important contribution to student success, as well as restructuring movements calling for increased levels of parental involvement. According to Christenson, Rounds, and Gorney (1992), *"Parent involvement...is defined broadly to include various activities that allow parents to participate in the educational process at school and at home"* (p. 190; italics added). Chavkin and Williams (1985) suggest that parent involvement is "any of a variety of activities that allow parents to participate in the educational process at home or in school, such as information exchange, decision sharing, volunteer services for schools, home tutoring/teaching, and child advocacy" (p. 2). Concrete examples of parent involvement include parents' volunteering to help in the school's computer lab and parents attending annual "Back to School" nights.

Home–school collaboration is a term often used synonymously with parent involvement; however, collaboration stresses the complementary relationship between families and educators. According to Christenson and Cleary (1990), it "refers to addressing parents' and teachers' concerns about children, engaging in problem solving...to resolve educational problems, and establishing a partnership" (p. 226). An example of this approach is to have parents meet with teachers and a consultant to identify specific problems a child is having, mutually develop a program to address the concerns, and share in the responsibility for implementating the program.

Joyce Epstein has conducted extensive research in the area of parent involvement and home–school collaboration, and has offered a conceptual framework comprised of five types of programs. First, there are basic obligations that families must provide to prepare their children for learning (e.g., health, supportive home conditions). Second, schools also assume basic obligations such as communication about school activities and programs. Third, parents can become actively involved at school through volunteer programs or attendance at school functions. A fourth type of involvement requests parents to engage in learning activities at home, such as monitoring homework or enhancing classroom work with examples from the "real world." Finally, parents can become involved in school governance and assist in schoolwide decision making (Epstein, 1987). Recently, Epstein and Dauber (1991) suggested a sixth type of parent involvement, calling for increased collaboration among schools, families, and community agencies.

Benefits of Parent Involvement

When parents are involved in their children's education, their children do better in school and go to better schools (Henderson, 1987). Parent involvement has been a central component of programs designed to improve educational outcomes for children at risk for school failure (Comer, 1984; Nye, 1989), to enhance the social development of students (Comer & Haynes, 1991), and to improve the academic performance of handicapped learners in the regular classroom (Wang, Gennari, & Waxman, 1985).

Reviews of the parent involvement literature suggest that parent participation in school affairs is related to increased student achievement, better school attendance, better study habits, fewer discipline problems, more positive attitudes toward school, more regular homework habits, greater similarity between the school and family, and a greater degree of familiarity between the teacher and family (Becher, 1986; Epstein, 1984). Parents report that when they participate in collaborative home–school efforts, they communicate better with the school and are more willing to help with educational tasks (Christenson & Cleary, 1990; Epstein, 1987, 1991; Stevenson & Baker, 1987). Teachers' frequent use of parent-involvement practices is also positively related to increased parental knowledge about the instructional program and parental ratings of teachers' interpersonal skills and professional merit (Epstein, 1986). Other benefits of active parent involvement include positive effects on students' attitudes toward school, homework, and perception of family and school ties (Epstein, 1982); improved parental understanding of schools; and increased opportunities for school staff and parents to share expertise (Jowett & Baginsky, 1988); as well as increased student achievement (Epstein, 1991) and higher student grades (Fehrmann, Keith, & Reimers, 1987).

Despite research support for parent involvement practices, the actual use of this potentially valuable resource has been limited. Becker and Epstein (1982) reported that many teachers question the success of practical efforts to involve parents in learning activities at home, citing lack of parental time and expertise. Teachers and school psychologists have reported that they are uncertain about how to involve parents and still maintain their roles as "professional experts." Time constraints also have been cited as reasons for lack of parent involvement (Fine, 1984; Sheridan & Kratochwill, 1991). Teachers' sense of self-efficacy seems to be one factor influencing the degree to which parents are involved in home–school collaboration. Teachers who believe that they are competent and performing a useful service are less likely to view parents as threatening and are more open to working with them to solve learning and behavioral problems (Hoover-Dempsey, Bassler, & Brissie, 1987; Power, 1985).

School practices of parent involvement emerge as more important factors than race, parent education, family size, marital status, and grade level in determining the degree of parent involvement in children's education. Most parents, including single parents and working parents, want to know how to help their children at home and how to stay involved in their children's education (Epstein, 1990, in press; Epstein & Scott-Jones, 1988). In fact, most parents help their children with school-related tasks at home, but many do not know whether they are doing the right thing or doing things right (Dauber & Epstein, 1989).

In sum, parent involvement is considered by many to be an essential variable in improving the likelihood that interventions to solve school problems will be maximally effective. Despite this general acknowledgment, psychologists often have not included parents as critical elements in the behavior change process, thus wasting a potentially valuable resource (Kramer, 1990a). The use of a systematic method of involving parents in active problem resolution may be especially important for children with severe or intractable academic or behavioral problems, as such difficulties often have far-reaching implications for children's later adjustment. Behavioral consultation can provide the needed structure and empirical support for involving parents in their children's education.

RECOMMENDATIONS FOR WORKING WITH PARENTS

Establishing and maintaining effective, reciprocal relationships with parents can be a challenging, ongoing process. Home–school partnerships require effort on the part of both parents and professionals. Fostering trust and open communication are among the keys to working with parents. The school atmosphere generally sets the stage for effective and productive relations with parents. When trying to solicit the active involvement of all families, it is important that the school atmosphere be open, positive, and facilitative. Other principles for parent consultation are presented in Table 2.1.

Table 2.1. Principles of Effective Parent Consultation

1. Complete preconsultation preparations, such as reviewing records and communicating with parents (i.e., set a convenient time for both parents to attend, give directions to the meeting location if necessary, check for special needs, provide a reminder).
2. Reinforce parents for attending meetings.
3. Demonstrate an interest in parents as people.
4. Demonstrate competence, caring, and interest in the child.
5. Acknowledge and validate parents' existing attempts to solve the problem.
6. Attend to the affective responses of parents using effective interviewing and listening skills.
7. Avoid criticizing or blaming parents.
8. Give constructive feedback without appearing condescending toward the parents.
9. Use humor appropriately.
10. Solicit parents' ideas about the causes of and solutions for problems.
11. Focus on competencies of the child.
12. Link intervention goals to future developmental tasks for parents and the child.
13. Use expert knowledge to provide information in a comprehensible way.
14. Provide a rationale for tasks and ideas to aid understanding.
15. Be an advocate for the child.

Source: Adapted from Sanders, M. R., & Dadds, M. R. (1993). *Behavioral family intervention*. Boston: Allyn & Bacon. Reproduced with permission.

Consultants and other school personnel should monitor carefully their messages to individual parents. Important aspects of messages include both the *nature of statements* (the actual words used) and the *manner in which they are delivered* (the tone, openness, and sincerity conveyed). Obviously, these aspects often overlap to impart an especially positive or negative message to parents (Welch & Sheridan, 1995). Unfortunately, teachers, administrators, or consultants may say things to parents that are insensitive, defensive, or unintended. For example, the following type of comment may be too familiar to some parents: "Your child won't ever be able to make it in the fourth grade!" Statements such as this may have the effect of alienating parents or widening the gap between them and the school. It is important to remember that most parents have strong emotional and psychological investment in their child, and demeaning comments are often taken personally.

One way of monitoring communications to parents is to approach every interaction as a potential "win–win" situation, rather than a "win–lose" confrontation. This statement means that *each* interaction between parents and school personnel should be inviting and open. Take, for example, a parent who approaches a teacher and claims, "You're not giving Stan enough time to finish his work!" A defensive response might be, "Well, Stan is the lowest in the class and I can't keep the other kids behind! There are 25 other students in the class, you know." Contrast this statement to an open response such as, "I can see you're concerned about Stan's learning. Let's take a look at where he is and decide how together we can meet his needs."

When interacting with parents, it is important that there be communication be both ways. Thus, consultants must be good listeners. Active listening skills can be remembered with the acronym CAPS (Welch & Sheridan, 1995), which stands for Clarifying, Attending, Paraphrasing, and Summarizing.

Clarifying is important to ensure that parents understand exactly what is meant by statements. Specific and concrete examples help clarify messages for parents. For example, if a teacher or consultant would like Peter's father to understand that Peter has difficulty playing cooperatively with other students, actual observations made during a 30-minute recess period might be described (e.g., Peter pushed three children during recess, threw a ball at a peer with force, and threatened to destroy another student's electronic game). These types of concrete statements with specific behavioral referents are more clear than a statement such as, "Your child has poor social skills!"

Attending is the second active listening skill and includes the SHARE behaviors (Sit squarely; Have an open posture, Acknowledge parents' statements; Relax; use Eye communication). The main advantage of attending is that it conveys to parents the message that you care about what they are saying and that you want to understand their viewpoint.

Paraphrasing is the third component of effective listening and involves restating in one's own words the main points of a parent's statement. For example, Kelly's mother might describe numerous issues associated with Kelly's homework completion (e.g., she refuses to begin homework, does not know the assignments, fails to have the necessary books or tools, and works sporadically). An appropriate paraphrase in this example might be, "It sounds like homework is a difficult time at your house, as Kelly tries very hard to avoid it altogether."

Summarizing is the final active listening skill. It is extremely important to use summarizing with parents, as it pulls together several key points of a discussion and ensures that all participants understand and agree upon what was said. Summarizing also strengthens communications by emphasizing those issues in need of attention.

Advanced relationship-building skills are also important when interacting with parents. These skills can be remembered with the acronym GRACE, which denotes the necessity to manifest Genuineness, Reflection, Acceptance, Concreteness, and Empathy (Welch & Sheridan, 1995). These skills are critical to promote an atmosphere of respect and openness to parents. They convey the message that parents are worthwhile and valued in consultation relationships.

Several additional recommendations for establishing effective relationships with families are available in other sources. Interested readers are referred to texts by Christenson and Conoley (1992), Henderson, Marburger, and Ooms (1986), Kanfer and Goldstein (1986), Swap (1993), and Welch and Sheridan (1995) for further information.

DISCUSSION QUESTIONS

1	Why is it important to involve parents in consultation?
2	What are some of the positive "side effects" of parent involvement (effects that were not planned, but that occur as an outcome of working with parents)? What might be some negative side effects?
3	What are some situations where parent education services might be warranted? In what situations would parent training be the intervention of choice? When might parent consultation be the most appropriate approach?

4   What factors might affect the success of parent involvement programs? How might programs differ in an inner-city school compared to a suburban or rural school?

5   What are some signs of parental defensiveness and resistance? What are some possible strategies to decrease defensiveness and resistance and increase parental support and involvement?

Conceptual Bases of Conjoint Behavioral Consultation

Upon completing this chapter, readers should be able to:

1. Describe the major principles of behavior theory, systems theory, and ecological theory.
2. Define conjoint behavioral consultation.
3. Outline the various assumptions of conjoint behavioral consultation.
4. State several advantages of conjoint behavioral consultation.
5. List the outcome and process goals of conjoint behavioral consultation.
6. Articulate important issues that consultants must consider when conducting conjoint behavioral consultation.

INTRODUCTION

Conjoint behavioral consultation represents an expansion of traditional behavioral consultation by promoting a coordinated and cooperative problem-solving relationship between parents and professionals. This chapter (1) presents various theoretical frameworks that contribute to our conceptualization of conjoint behavioral consultation (i.e., behavioral theory, systems theory, and ecological theory), (2) defines conjoint behavioral consultation, and (3) explores various assumptions, advantages, goals, and practical considerations.

BEHAVIORAL THEORY

There are many underlying assumptions of behavioral theory. First, the theory rests firmly on the assumption that behaviors are learned as a function of their interaction with the environment. Approaches that derive from behavioral theory, then, rely on specific techniques that use learning principles to constructively change human behavior. Likewise, behavioral approaches focus on observable behaviors of a child, parent, and teacher, rather than some underlying cause. They emphasize the reciprocal interactions among individuals and the environmental variables that maintain specific behavior patterns. Given the emphasis on specific behaviors, behavior therapy involves setting specific and clearly defined intervention goals. Rather than being concerned with underlying causes of a behavior or "personality traits," the emphasis is on the "here and now" and identifying relevant environmental conditions that may be contributing to a given situation. Finally, there is a great deal of emphasis placed on obtaining empirical support for various treatment techniques, including objective documentation of treatment effects for individual subjects.

Over the years, some limitations of behavior therapy have been identified, and this process has set the stage for the expansion of the theory and practice. In traditional behavioral therapy, the focus is on analyzing a given problem molecularly, without addressing the broader context within which it occurs. Traditional behavioral assessment methods that focus on a single treatment target behavior in one setting are generally inadequate in assessing interrelationships within environmental contexts. Likewise, traditional behavioral therapists do not typically consider intervention side effects (Petrie et al., 1980). This being the case, behavioral consultants may interact with consultees in such a way that environmental variables become conceptualized in a "sequential, molecular, temporally constricted and contextually ignorant fashion" (Witt & Martens, 1988, p. 213).

Given these considerations, some behavioral therapists have called for expansion of the assessment paradigm. For example, behavioral consultants have traditionally considered only those stimulus events that immediately precede and follow the target behavior. This temporal constriction can cause difficulties in both the functional analysis and the measurement of behavior (Cataldo, 1984). It is often desirable to investigate events that are temporally or contextually distal to a target behavior, yet functionally related to its occurrence. *Setting events* refer to temporally or contextually removed stimuli that bear a functional relation to behavior (Wahler & Fox, 1981). These setting events may be of a physical, social, or affective nature. Behavioral assessment should go beyond immediate conditions and consider a more holistic view of a situation, including ecological considerations and setting events (Lentz & Shapiro, 1986; Wahler & Fox, 1981; Ysseldyke & Christenson, 1987).

In analyzing a problem situation, environmental context must also be considered (Gresham & Noell, 1993; Gresham & Kendell, 1987). Behavior may be best conceptualized as a function of contingent reinforcement for a particular behavior and also of all other reinforcement operating in the environment at a given time. Thus, a behavioral/functional analysis of the conditions maintaining a target behavior is necessary. Determination of the current contingencies and behavioral history of a presenting problem can greatly affect the potential success and long-term maintenance of a behavioral program.

The focus of traditional behavioral therapy and behavioral consultation has been on the identification, analysis, and remediation of child (client) problems. However, the consultant should consider a broad environmental context. Specifically, behavioral consultants should try to fully address the complex interactions and interdependencies among individual, classroom, culture, family, and community on the educational process (Christenson, Abery, & Weinberg, 1986; Knoff, 1984). In this way, a more complete picture of schools and schooling may be obtained than if a limited context is analyzed. What is needed is an understanding of broader ecological conditions within which behaviors occur, including the pervasive relationships among one's behavior, the environment, and significant others.

SYSTEMS THEORY

Systems theory has been presented as the philosophical foundation for describing behaviors and interactions within and between families and schools (Conoley, 1987a). The primary assumption of systems theory is that individual dysfunction is symptomatic of structural and interactional difficulties in a larger system (i.e., the family or the classroom system) (Minuchin, 1974; Minuchin & Fishman, 1981). The family (or classroom) is perceived as a dynamic system, with each component contributing to the maintenance of the entire system. According to systems theory, a child's "problem" does not reside within the child or exclusively in the child's environment. Rather, a behavior occurs as a function of the interaction of the child with the systems of which the child is a part.

Early systems theorists emphasized the "family" as the primary system of which the child is a component. However, this may be a rather limited focus given the current nature of society and nontraditional family structures that exist today. According to early family systems theory, children establish their identity through the interplay of roles and relationships within the family system (Fine & Holt, 1983). The parts of a system are interconnected, and therefore change in one part of a system affects other parts. Likewise, children transcend systems (e.g., home, school, and peer groups) and become involved in several systems. Each system involves relationship, power, and communication structures, and there are explicit and implicit rules within systems that guide behavior. The systems overlap, and what occurs in one system affects the child's behaviors in other systems. For example, McDaniel (1981) described a child who adapted well to a chaotic home, but the behaviors that were adaptive in the home setting (i.e., attention seeking) reportedly alienated his teachers at school.

In family systems theory, the family rather than the individual is the target of treatment. The goal of treatment is to change not only the "patient's" behavior, but also the dysfunctional family system that maintains the behavior. Although the systems perspective has traditionally been conceptualized as a family-oriented therapeutic approach, the utilization of such a perspective to better understand school dynamics has been advocated by a number of writers, who argue that family systems have far-reaching implications in the effectiveness of classroom instruction (Conoley, 1987b; Fine & Holt, 1983; Fish & Jain, 1988; Power & Bartholomew, 1985). In an early publication, Friedman (1969) emphasized the impact of the family on school learning and recognized that "the patterns of socialization and learning are first acquired in the family setting and the parents of the child are his first teachers" (p. 162). He advocated using a structured interview with parents to determine how family dynamics affect the child in school.

Fine and Holt (1983) offered an appealing extension of the family systems perspective to the school setting. These authors argued that viewing a child's school behavior from a systems perspective allows the consultant an expanded perception of the contextual function of behavior. They provided examples of how the school-based consultant can intervene from a systems perspective, using interviews, short-term family intervention, and teacher consultation, with an implicit suggestion that the consultant call together the family and school personnel for the initial interview to view the child's "systems in action."

Authors in a miniseries in *School Psychology Review* (1987, Vol. 16) presented several roles for promoting direct and indirect involvement by school psychologists to address parent and family needs. The traditional role of the school psychologist was expanded to encompass systemic family assessment (Paget, 1987), structured family therapy (Carlson, 1987), strategic family intervention (Conoley, 1987a), family empowerment (Dunst & Trivette, 1987), and multiple family group therapy (Dombalis & Erchul,

1987). Although most authors acknowledged the importance of home–school relations, only Power and Bartholomew (1987) presented an in-depth discussion of family–school relationship patterns and the complex interactions within and between these systems.

Difficulties arise when applying a systemic approach to school consultation. One issue is that of the identification and definition of the client system. Traditionally, systems theory encompassed the family-as-system as the appropriate "patient" in therapy. However, when the consultant views the client system as the child in interaction with the teacher, the family, and the home and school environments, the consultative relationship is qualitatively different.

Although some guidelines are provided for the clinician who utilizes a systemic approach, the procedures are generally descriptive and nonstandardized. This format may present difficulties for the psychologist working with the family and school collaboratively, in that specific roles and responsibilities are less well-defined and specific problem-solving procedures may be complex and ambiguous. While most therapists conclude that their methods are effective, specific procedural information is lacking. This issue becomes particularly problematic when replication in research is attempted. Behavioral approaches, as we have noted, are more conducive to standardized procedures, and they generally provide objective observational data to verify changes in the individual's or family's functioning.

ECOLOGICAL THEORY

Ecological theory is concerned with the interaction between an individual and the environment. Instead of focusing only on individuals, ecological theorists generally examine ecosystems or the interactions among systems. Whereas strict behavior analysts typically focus on a narrow and unique portion of the context within which a person and behavior are embedded, ecological theorists consider interdependencies between two behaviors, two settings, and a behavior and the setting (Gump, 1977). Likewise, ecologists typically engage in naturalistic research to understand human behavior in its natural setting.

The ecological approach conceptualizes development as a "mutual accommodation" between an individual and the environment. Central to ecological theory is the assumption that each child is an inseparable part of a small social system. By this assumption, development occurs in the context of four interrelated systems within the ecological environment (Bronfenbrenner, 1977). The *microsystem* consists of the relation between the child and the child's immediate setting (e.g., home, school). According to ecological theory, however, one must look beyond the microsystem to the relations and linkages between and among microsystems. In other words, one must also consider the child's *mesosystem*, or the interrelations among the major settings and systems in the child's life (e.g., interactions between the home and school, or between the child's parents and the child's peer group). *Exosystem* influences are events in settings in which the child does not directly participate, but that impinge upon or encompass the immediate settings in which the child is involved (e.g., events at a parent's workplace or in a teacher's home life). Finally, the *macrosystem* comprises the overall cultural and subcultural patterns of society (e.g., broad economic, political, and legal systems; values and traditions within a community).

A child's mesosystem may be of particular interest to the consultant working with parents and school personnel. The interconnections among systems presumably have a significant impact on development. Just as influences within families and schools are reciprocal, influences between them are reciprocal; a child's school experiences influence the child's experiences and behavior at home, and family experiences influence school behavior and performance (Conoley, 1987a; Hansen, 1986).

Hansen (1986) illustrated the importance of mesosystemic relationships in his analysis of forms of interaction rules between families and schools. He paid particular attention to mismatches in the ways family members and classroom participants relate to one another and found that the greater the discontinuity in interaction rules between home and school, the more the child's academic grades declined. It was concluded that a child's relationships outside the classroom influence both classroom competencies and participation in classroom interactions.

Several advantages are apparent in the use of ecological theory as a basis for family–school intervention. First, it extends traditional behavioral theory by emphasizing the reciprocal interactions among a behavior, person, and setting. Second, it goes beyond general systems theory to recognize the importance of the interrelations among various systems in a child's life. Furthermore, it theoretically subsumes other theories and is not likely to be inconsistent or incompatible with other theoretical systems used by practitioners (C. Anderson, 1983; Apter & Conoley, 1984). According to C. Anderson (1983), "as an umbrella theory, [ecological theory] allows an integration of sources of information and influence in the service of understanding child development" (p. 182).

Implications of Ecological Theory

Specific implications of ecological theory are apparent. First, to be effective, diagnosis and treatment of children must be more comprehensive and functional than they have been in the past. It is beneficial to gather data from as many sources as possible and to attempt to remain inclusive rather than exclusive with regard to the information that is utilized in the delivery of services to children.

A second implication of ecological systems theory stresses the importance of looking at the entire system surrounding each child. Understanding the concerns of significant others (i.e., parents, teachers) in the child's environment is equally important. The coordination of these significant others is critical. Linkages between various aspects of each child's world are seen as critical in the development of successful programs (Apter, 1982).

The implications of ecological assessment and intervention also deserve attention. Ecological assessment strategies represent efforts to utilize more information in the development of effective programs. Focusing all attention on the child while ignoring the family, school, and community can make the identification and remediation of difficulties problematic. Likewise, ecological interventions can have a broad positive impact that will benefit others as well as the "target" child.

In ecological assessment, an effort is generally made to synthesize information from a variety of social situations in which the child exists. It begins with the broad perspective that views problems as system-centered, rather than individual-centered. The individual is seen in a context. From an ecological perspective, a consultant should strive to understand the network of interrelationships among various individuals and their environment (Apter, 1982). When appropriate, the focus may be on the individual, but always considering that the individual is part of systems that cannot be understood without reference to those systems. Ecological researchers attempt to assess children's interactions in the many environments (such as the home and school) that make up a child's ecosystem. Thus, potentially new and different information is brought into the planning process. Consistent with behavioral assessment tactics, useful methods include direct observations, interviews, and self-reports.

Both ecological and behavioral theorists acknowledge that intervention must take place in the child's natural environment, generally within the home setting and major social institutions such as the school. Significant individuals within the child's social network should be utilized as agents of change. Any form of intervention has limited value unless it takes into account significant social/ecological factors and uses them for the maintenance of change. The general goal of an ecological intervention is increased concordance between the behavior of the child and the setting(s) in which the child resides. Ecological interventions may be borrowed from many disciplines, but are implemented in the context of a broad and comprehensive ecological format.

Ecological Theory and Consultation

Ecological theory emphasizes the essential need to increase one's ability to work effectively with the significant adults in a child's life. Parents, teachers, and school personnel are all intertwined in a child's ecosystem. Coordination of such persons can be critical in the remediation of difficulties. The provision of indirect services (i.e., consultative interventions with the goal of improving the identified child's situation) may be especially appropriate.

Methods of coordinating significant adults in a child's life and of "building bridges" between home and school have been described (Apter & Conoley, 1984; Conoley, 1987b). For example, Conoley (1987b) suggested four levels of intervention with increasing degrees of permeability across home and school boundaries. The function of Level 1 interventions is to share information between home and school primarily through the use of report cards, phone calls, and infrequent parent–teacher meetings. Level 2 interventions involve collaborative home–school programs with all parties understanding clearly the expectations of each, the establishment of feasible communication systems between all parties, and consistent follow-through on the part of teachers and parents. Interventions at Level 3 entail active involvement of parents in the school setting, with the intent of reducing discontinuities between home and school. The final phase of home–school partnership (Level 4) involves the reciprocal education of parents and teachers by each other. Additional conceptual and operational models for working with parents were presented in Chapter 2.

Given the assumptions of ecological theory, it follows that family involvement in a cooperative educational plan is essential. Accordingly, the critical element is cooperation between the home and school for facilitating adaptive student behavior. The key components of a cooperative plan include (1) agreement on some target behavioral changes between teacher, parents, and child, if possible; (2) a feasible communication method between the two systems; and (3) consistent follow-through on the part of teachers and parents in terms of providing the agreed-upon rewards (Apter & Conoley, 1984).

To promote effective home–school partnerships, clear and operational procedures should be available to guide one through the process of implementing services. Unfortunately, such procedural guidelines are unavailable in the ecological-systems literature. Further, little empirical evidence exists that articulates the efficacy of these theoretical approaches in consultation. Therefore, ecological and systems theories are presented as a framework to guide conceptualization of a broader consultation approach. There is a need for further research to investigate the contribution of these theories to consultation practice. Behavioral theory, and behavioral consultation in particular, provides a useful, empirically documented framework for working within (and potentially between) systems to effect change (Bergan & Kratochwill, 1990; Kratochwill & Bergan, 1990). The structured problem-solving approach (see Chapter 1) may be particularly effective in linking parent and school resources in a conjoint, collaborative process.

CONJOINT BEHAVIORAL CONSULTATION

To facilitate collaborative partnerships among significant individuals in a child's life, simultaneous consultation with parents and teachers is a promising approach. From this perspective, conjoint rather than parallel (i.e., teacher-only or parent-only) consultation is necessary. Conjoint behavioral consultation is defined as "*a structured, indirect form of service-delivery, in which parents and teachers are joined to work together to address the academic, social, or behavioral needs of an individual for whom both parties bear some responsibility*" (Sheridan & Kratochwill, 1992, p. 122). It is designed to engage significant consultees from various systems in a collaborative problem-solving process. In this model, the interconnections between systems are considered critically important. A structural model of conjoint behavioral consultation, emphasizing the reciprocal, interacting systems in a child's life, is depicted in Figure 3.1.

It can be noted that the systems depicted in Figure 3.1 go beyond the home and school. Indeed, any system with which the child or family interacts can be a participant in conjoint behavioral consultation. These may include extended family members, alternative caregivers, clergy, support service personnel, probation officers, therapists, or a host of others who have regular and meaningful contact with the child. Such individuals may provide additional information about the problem, as well as meaningful observations that can contribute to an accurate functional analysis. Further, they can serve as additional resources when delineating intervention strategies and tactics. The inclusion of participants across these various systems can also ensure cross-setting consistency in

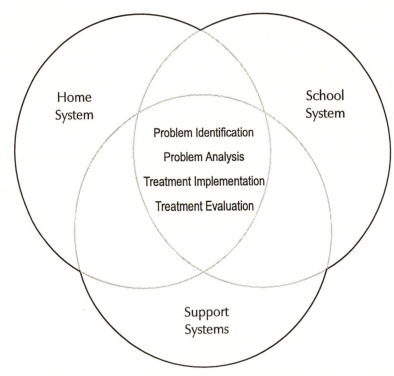

Figure 3.1. Structural model of conjoint behavioral consultation. (*Source*: Adapted from an earlier model that first appeared in Sheridan, S. M., & Kratochwill, T. R. [1991]. Behavioral consultation in applied settings. In J. W. Lloyd, A. C. Repp, & N. N. Singh [Eds.], *The regular education initiative: Alternative perspectives on concepts, issues, and methods* (pp. 193–210). Pacific Grove, CA: Brooks/Cole.)

treatment implementation and maximize maintenance and generalization of treatment effects. Clearly, the addition of more individuals in consultation can complicate the process; however, the benefits of a comprehensive approach clearly outweigh the costs. Readers are referred to Conoley and Sheridan (in press) for an example of an "expanded" conjoint behavioral consultation model with children who have experienced a traumatic brain injury.

Assumptions

Several assumptions must be made when establishing collaborative home–school relations through conjoint consultation. The main assumption is that children, families, and schools are viewed from an ecological behavioral perspective. The home–school relationship must be viewed as a cooperative and interactive partnership, as compared to one that is separate and isolated. Furthermore, shared implication in a problem and its resolution is assumed to maximize commitment to program goals, including the overarching social and educational goals of school settings.

In conjoint behavioral consultation, it is further assumed that collaborative problem solving will afford the greatest benefits. All persons are recognized as possessing important knowledge and skills, and it is necessary that parents and teachers be willing and open to share information, learn from each other, value each other's input, and incorporate each other's insights into possible interventions. Pooling information, sharing resources, obtaining clear conceptualizations of problems, and increasing the range and superiority of solutions are among the primary objectives of a conjoint consultation experience.

Advantages

There are several advantages of conjoint behavioral consultation. First, it represents a conceptual expansion of traditional consultation, with a focus on the interacting systems within a child's life. A simultaneous, conjoint model extends earlier consultation work by providing services to parents and teachers *together.* Second, by actively joining parents and teachers in a structured problem-solving framework, comprehensive and systematic data can be collected on the child's behavior over time and across settings. Data collection over time and across settings may help identify various events that may be functionally related to, but removed in time and place from, target behaviors (i.e., setting events) (Wahler & Fox, 1981). Third, consistent programming across settings may enhance generalization and maintenance of consultation treatment effects (Drabman, Hammer, & Rosenbaum, 1979). Finally, involving significant treatment agents across settings can help monitor the occurrence of intervention effects that were unplanned or undesirable (Kazdin, 1982).

Goals

The conceptual and procedural extensions represented in conjoint behavioral consultation present several goals and objectives in addition to those articulated in more traditional approaches to consultation. In this service-delivery model, it is first hoped that consultants and consultees will recognize the need to address problems as occurring across, rather than within, settings. Second, it is expected that consultees will share joint responsibility for problem identification and resolution. A third goal is improved communication and interaction among the child, family, and school personnel. Fourth, by expanding the assessment base, a comprehensive and functional understanding of identified problems should be possible. A fifth goal is consistency among change agents in behavioral interventions, promoting transfer and maintenance of treatment effects across settings. Sixth, improved functioning on the part of all parties (i.e., family members, school personnel, and the child-client) is anticipated. A seventh goal is the development of skills and competencies to promote future independent conjoint problem solving between the family and school personnel. These and additional process and outcome goals of conjoint behavioral consultation are presented in Table 3.1.

Table 3.1. Process and Outcome Goals of Conjoint Behavioral Consultation

Process Goals

1. Increase communication and knowledge about family (e.g., family history, medical information, prior treatments).
2. Improve relationship among the child, family (mother and father), and school personnel.
3. Establish home-school partnership.
4. Promote shared ownership for problem definition and solution.
5. Increase parent (mother and father) and teacher commitments to educational goals.
6. Recognize the need to address problems as occurring across, rather than within, settings.
7. Promote greater conceptualization of a problem.
8. Increase the diversity of expertise and resources available.

Outcome Goals

1. Obtain comprehensive and functional data over extended temporal and contextual bases.
2. Establish consistent treatment programs across settings.
3. Improve the skills, knowledge, and behaviors of all parties (i.e., family members, school personnel, and the child-client).
4. Monitor behavioral contrast and side effects systematically via cross-setting treatment agents.
5. Enhance generalization and maintenance of treatment effects via consistent programming across sources and settings.
6. Develop skills and competencies to promote further independent conjoint problem-solving between the family and school personnel.

Source: Sheridan, S. M., & Kratochwill, T. R. (1992). Behavioral parent–teacher consultation: Conceptual and research considrations. *Journal of School Psychology*, *30*, 117–139. Reproduced with permission.

Several interpersonal and procedural considerations are necessary to maximize the effectiveness of consultation. Initially, it is important to establish rapport with consultees. Relationship building is an important consideration in all forms of consultation; however, this component may present an especially complex situation when more than one consultee is involved and when the several consultees represent different systems in a child's life. Throughout the consultation process, every effort must be made to promote positive work relations among parents and teachers and between the consultant and the interacting subsystems. It is especially important to consider the interpersonal dynamics operating at all levels (i.e., between parents and teachers; consultant and consultees; and parents, teacher, consultant, and client).

Parent involvement in consultation provides the opportunity to obtain important information regarding child- and family-related factors, including family history and various child characteristics (e.g., disposition, medical history, developmental milestones). Such information is often relevant and necessary for a consultant to develop a complete understanding of a case. At times, however, parents may be uncomfortable discussing such events with school professionals. Respect of family privacy is important to maximize ongoing involvement, so it is important that consultants recognize personal desires of parents regarding their communication with school personnel. When such information is considered necessary for effective consultation, a separate meeting or interview between the consultant and parents prior to conjoint consultation sessions may be required.

Along with child and family characteristics, history of problem-solving efforts on the part of parents and teachers, previous parent–teacher interactions, severity of problems across settings, and prior intervention efforts may affect consultation outcome. The consultant must be sensitive to these historical, interpersonal, and case-related variables throughout the consultative process. In cases where extreme negative relations impede the ability to form a collaborative partnership, the consultant may begin by working simultaneously with parents and teachers and gradually work toward establishing a productive working relationship among all parties.

In conjoint consultation, the involvement of more than one consultee may present a challenge to the consultant who is attempting to obtain comprehensive information in a focused, systematic manner. The structured forms presented in the Appendix may lend themselves to an overly rigid and stoic interviewing style, particularly for individuals learning the model.

It is important to remember that the forms are only tools with which the consultant can gather necessary information in a logical format. However, *skillful interviewing is more than simply covering a predetermined list of potentially relevant questions or topics.* It is a fluid process of continuously eliciting information and generating and testing hypotheses regarding the nature of a problem and conditions maintaining its occurrence (Sanders & Dadds, 1993).

Active participation and commitment of all participants, respect for and openness to each individual's expertise, open communication, and the use of effective conflict management strategies are essential in all forms of consultation, including that conducted with parents and teachers together. All participants also must be clear about each individual's role and responsibilities to maximize consultation effectiveness. Therefore, parents and teachers should be informed of the purpose, procedures, and potential benefits and limitations of conjoint behavioral consultation. It is important to clarify responsibilities of all parties and review procedural details early in the consultation process. For example, joint meetings of the parent(s), teacher(s), and consultant are the structural cornerstone of conjoint behavioral consultation, and the importance of working collaboratively in consultation sessions should be highlighted. The notions of shared participation in problem identification and resolution, open and increased communication between parents and teachers, and consistency in interventions between home and school should also be emphasized. The need for data collection, home and school observations, and possible consultee training are additional procedural details that should be discussed.

CONSULTANT AND CONSULTEE POINTS OF VIEW IN CONJOINT BEHAVIORAL CONSULTATION

The points of view that participants bring to consultation take on a different meaning in conjoint behavioral consultation than was the case in early forms of consultation and therapy. Historically in psychotherapy, the therapist was assumed to possess special knowledge of the truth not necessarily shared by the patient. For example, within Freud's psychoanalytic theory, when the therapist and patient expressed things in different ways, the patient was often labeled as defensive (e.g., Freud, 1927, 1938). Defensiveness was assumed to prevent the patient from seeing the truth as it was understood by the therapist. Several different defense mechanisms were identified that described the various reactions that prevented patients from discerning the true state of affairs (e.g., Freud, 1927, 1938). A similar line of reasoning has been advanced with respect to consultation services. In the case of consultation, the term "resistance" is often used to describe differences in point of view between the consultant and consultee (e.g., Wickstrom & Witt, 1993). For example, consider the familiar situation in which a consultant is providing services to a teacher (consultee) who is concerned about a problem manifested by a child in the classroom setting. The consultant may assume that the problem can be solved in the classroom if an appropriate intervention is designed and if the teacher implements the intervention. The teacher, on the other hand, may feel that the quickest and easiest way to solve the problem is to remove the child from the class. Under conditions such as these, consultants often use the term resistance to label the teachers' point of view (e.g., Wickstrom & Witt, 1993). Various techniques have been suggested for dealing with resistance, and these techniques appear to show promise for increasing the effectiveness of consultation services (Wickstrom & Witt, 1993).

Another way to look at the issues associated with the concept of resistance is to conceptualize the participants in consultation as each coming to the consultation process with a point of view. The points of view represented in consultation may be similar in some respects and different in others. When there are differences that appear to impede the implementation of consultation, the consultant may choose to label them as forms of resistance. However, it is important to recognize that such a label has the effect of giving special weight to the consultant's point of view and perhaps by implication denigrating the consultee's point of view. With the involvement of two consultees and one consultant in conjoint behavioral consultation, at least three potentially unique points of view may be represented.

There are good reasons for assuming that consultants are in the right and that consultees are resistant to services. Consultants have specialized training and experience that may give them an advantage in determining most accurately the state of affairs in a given case. For example, it is the consultant's responsibility to bring his or her expert knowledge of the science of psychology to bear on the formulation and solution of problems presented by the consultee (Bergan & Kratochwill, 1990). This expert knowledge may lead the consultant to adopt a point of view about a case that is different from the view taken by consultees. Nonetheless, the collegial perspective inherent in consultation suggests the usefulness of avoiding the assumption that the consultant's point of view should be given special weight.

The collegial perspective implies that equal weight should be given to each participant's point of view. Given the assumption of equal weight, the resolution of differences may require a full and open exploration of *each* participant's point of view (including both the parent's and teacher's). This exploration should reveal the consequences of each point of view in ways that fully explore the risks and benefits associated with the various courses of action inherent in each point of view. For example, to encourage exploration of a consultee's point of view, a consultant might say: "What are the benefits for George of not trying to solve this problem in the classroom?" Discussion might then proceed to a discussion of risks. Exploration of the consultee's point of view may be accompanied by a full discussion of the consultant's views on the matter. The consultant may wish to point out the perceived benefits of his or her view and the risks and constraints associated with the view. The goal of such exploration is to arrive at common ground that will make it possible to proceed in ways that will solve the problems to be addressed in consultation.

In order for consultation to proceed, there must be common agreement with respect to certain issues. For example, there must be agreement that there is a problem to be solved and a shared willingness to implement a problem-solving process to achieve a solution. When there is disagreement on these fundamentals, consultation is not the procedure of choice for providing services to the client.

INDICATIONS AND CONTRAINDICATIONS OF THE MODEL ━━━━━━━

Like any form of consultation or service-delivery model, conjoint behavioral consultation is not a panacea. It may not be appropriate for all cases in all circumstances. There will be many situations when consultation with parents and teachers together is highly recommended. One such example is when a child's externalizing behavior problems permeate across the home and school settings, as is the case with many problems of noncompliance and aggression. Second, children who manifest skill deficits may benefit from a conjoint approach, because the parent and teacher can work toward teaching and reinforcing skills that can be used across settings. Third, some academic problems, such as difficulties completing homework, have behavioral manifestations both at home and at school. For example, at school the child may demonstrate poor organizational skills (such as failure to attend, failure to record assignments, or difficulty getting started working). At home, the child's organizational problems may be evidenced by poor study habits (such as distractibility, lack of proper supplies to complete homework, or avoidance behaviors). Although the component behaviors may not be identical across settings, a collaborative approach is clearly warranted in cases where the overall target (homework completion) has behavioral manifestations across settings. A third area that is particularly appropriate for conjoint behavioral consultation is the case wherein discontinuities between the home and school (Hansen, 1986) are apparent (e.g., inconsistent expectations for the student or variable approaches for addressing behavioral difficulties). In these cases, a mesosystemic target may be appropriate (such as improved communication, enhanced interactions, or increased structure or trust in the parent–teacher relationship). Keep in mind that targets at the mesosystemic level (i.e., those that deal with the home–school relationship) require operationalization to the same degree as do child-related targets.

There are some cases that suggest the inappropriateness of a conjoint behavioral consultation approach, at least in the initial stages of problem solving. First, some families may exhibit very dysfunctional patterns of interaction that serve to sabotage intervention efforts. These families may be best served by a family therapist who can address issues outside the school. Ideally, intensive family therapy may provide family members with needed structure and skills and empower them to be effective consultees at a later date (Sheridan & Kratochwill, 1992). Second, there may be situations where a teacher's negative disposition toward working with parents precludes the ability to form a trusting, collaborative relationship. Although this scenario is becoming less prevalent in education, there are still some educators who believe that the home and school settings should remain distinct. In these cases, the consultant may work individually with the teacher, provide similar examples where home–school collaboration was successful, and reinforce all statements that begin to support parental involvement. These and other influence strategies may be helpful in altering teacher attitudes. Third, cases where parents and teachers have experienced long-standing dissension to the point where extreme conflict and explosive interactions are inevitable will not benefit from this approach. In these cases, it is possible that a liaison between the two parties (such as a consultant) may be warranted. This individual may function as a positive ally for both individuals and as an advocate for the student. As positive communication and conflict management skills are modeled for parents and teachers, a plan may be arranged to begin some conjoint sessions and work toward establishing a productive home–school partnership (Sheridan & Kratochwill, 1992).

DISCUSSION QUESTIONS

1 | Why is an integrated theoretical approach to consultation useful when delivering services to parents and teachers in a conjoint fashion?

2 | What are some possible positive and negative side effects (effects that were not planned, but that occur as an outcome) of conjoint behavioral consultation?

3 | What important information about conjoint behavioral consultation might be shared with parents and teachers to increase clarity and effectiveness of the services?

4 | Are there some parents and teachers with whom conjoint behavioral consultation might be more or less feasible or appropriate? Why or why not?

5 | Practically speaking, what differences might you expect between consultation services delivered to a teacher or parent alone and those delivered in a conjoint fashion?

Stages of Conjoint Behavioral Consultation

CHAPTER OBJECTIVES

Upon completing this chapter, the reader should be able to:

1. Discuss methods for assessing family interactions.
2. Describe the role of functional assessment and analysis in conjoint behavioral consultation.
3. Outline the six goals of problem identification in conjoint behavioral consultation.
4. Define setting events and explain how they can be identified in conjoint behavioral consultation.
5. Explain the importance of treatment acceptability in conjoint behavioral consultation.
6. List the five goals of problem analysis in conjoint behavioral consultation.
7. Discuss the importance of and issues surrounding treatment integrity in conjoint behavioral consultation.
8. Identify important roles of consultants and consultees during treatment implementation.
9. State the four goals of treatment evaluation in conjoint behavioral consultation.

INTRODUCTION

In this chapter, we provide information on each of the stages of conjoint behavioral consultation. These stages generally mirror those in traditional behavioral consultation (Bergan & Kratochwill, 1990); however, the entire process is conducted with parents, teachers, and, in some cases, other significant individuals (e.g., extended family, additional service providers) *together.* Because of this format, there may be important differences in the manner in which each stage of consultation is practiced. Before beginning the process with consultees, it may be useful to assess (formally or informally) the home and school systems to determine whether a conjoint approach is warranted. Chapter 3 suggests several cases where collaborative problem solving may need to be postponed until certain personal or interpersonal issues can be addressed. If the approach is initiated, it is important to set the stage for effective consultation by reviewing the goals and objectives of the model, roles and responsibilities of all parties, and procedural details of the interviews, data collection procedures, and intervention and evaluation components (see Sheridan & Kratochwill, 1992).

STAGE 1: PROBLEM IDENTIFICATION

In the problem identification stage, the consultant and consultees work together to identify and clarify the most salient problem(s) to be targeted in consultation. In conjoint behavioral consultation, ecological variables that control client problems across settings are explored. Thus, target behaviors are identified in the context of situational conditions surrounding their occurrence across settings.

It is important to emphasize accurate and precise problem identification and definition in the consultation process. In conjoint consultation, a broad assessment base (i.e., incorporating diverse sources of information across settings) may assist in a complete and accurate analysis of the problem. Because data will be collected by several individuals across settings (i.e., parents, teachers, and possibly the child), different patterns of responding under various environmental conditions may be highlighted. A multisource, multisetting, multimethod assessment approach is necessary to clarify the target behavior. It is good consultation practice to utilize a number of assessment techniques across settings to aid in a comprehensive conceptualization of a student's difficulties. For example, rating scales, self-reports, sociometrics, and direct observations can be collected from various informants representing diverse settings to provide a breadth of information not available through interview data only (Kratochwill & Sheridan, 1990).

Family Assessment

In many cases, a comprehensive family and child assessment will be necessary prior to conjoint behavioral consultation. Among the major elements of the family assessment are (1) an initial interview, (2) direct observations, (3) self-report measures, and (4) completion of an ongoing functional analysis (Sanders & Dadds, 1993).

An *initial family interview* is often important for several reasons. First, as the initial point of contact with the family, it can be useful in establishing rapport. If the parents have been skeptical or uncertain about the school, they may begin to feel more at ease if they recognize the consultant as an ally among school staff. The interview can also allow for the identification of variables within the family's social and cultural contexts that may affect the child's development. It will also provide an opportunity to determine a parent's capacity to carry out an intervention program and can allow for early discussion of treatment goals. Guidelines for conducting an initial family interview are presented in Table 4.1. Some of the objectives of a family interview can be incorporated into the Conjoint Problem Identification Interview (e.g., discussing parents' primary concerns and clarifying difficulties, establishing a history and tentative topography of the primary problems). For confidentiality and brevity, other information (e.g., history of psychiatric conditions in other family members, information about family relationships) may be obtained in a brief family history with the parents prior to the initiation of consultation.

The child-client may be interviewed (usually separately from the parents) as part of the family interview. This interview may be useful for a number of reasons. First, children often have important ideas about the nature of the presenting problem. Second, if the target concern involves the child's subjective experiences (such as feelings, thoughts, or motivations), parental report may be inaccurate. Third, depending on the age and developmental level of the child, he or she may be the most accurate respondent on such issues regarding friendships and school experiences. Guidelines for conducting a child interview are in Table 4.2.

In some cases, the initial interview will suggest important environmental conditions related to the family's difficulties. *Direct observations* of family interaction allow the consultant to assess the broad ecological context surrounding presenting problems. When using direct observations as a means to assess family functioning, a structured interaction task procedure is useful (Sanders & Dadds, 1993). This procedure requires the consultant to provide family members with a task and instruct them to engage in the task. For example, if conflict management is a problem for a family, the consultant may ask them to complete the task of deciding where to go for dinner, what movie to rent at the video store, or any other task that is likely to cause disagreement. Ideally, the consultant will elicit problem behaviors from family members and have the opportunity to observe interaction patterns. The structured interac-

---

Table 4.1. Guidelines for Conducting an Initial Family Interview

---

1. Obtain identifying information (e.g., family demographic information such as number of children, ages, parent marital status, employment).
2. Establish the source of referral.
3. Discuss parents' main concerns about the child (i.e., presenting complaint)[a]:
   A. Begin with open-ended questions that give parents an opportunity to describe their concerns.
   B. Use follow-up questions to encourage elaboration on the nature of the complaint.
   C. Request examples to place the problem in context.
   D. Establish the approximate frequency, intensity, duration, and context of the problem.
4. Clarify other difficulties the child may have (i.e., associated problems)[a]:
   A. Explore the occurrence of problems that covary frequently with the main complaint.
   B. Summarize the main problem and request additional information on related behaviors.
5. Establish the history of the presenting complaint[a]:
   A. Ask about the approximate date of onset.
   B. Request information on the chronological development of symptoms.
6. Establish a tentative topography of presenting problems, to be clarified in consultation interviews[a]:
7. Explore the previous history of psychological or psychiatric help on the part of the child or other family members:
   A. Request information on the type of problem.
   B. Obtain specific information about previous help and interventions.
8. Elicit information on family history. Ask about:
   A. Family structure.
   B. Persons living in the home.
   C. Family history of psychiatric disturbance.
   D. Living and childcare arrangements.
   E. Financial or other family stressors.

---

tion task is useful for sampling a range of parent–child interactions because it allows for data to be collected in a short period of time, with attention to antecedents and consequences of behaviors.

Along with structured tasks, families can be asked to collect data on specific target behaviors at home. Behavioral occurrences, sequences, duration, or intensity can be recorded using simple or elaborate systems. When working with families, it is recommended that the procedures be very concrete, specific, and simple. A number of considerations for collecting direct observational data are included in Kratochwill and Sheridan (1990).

Self-report measures include both self-monitoring procedures and paper and pencil inventories. *Self-monitoring* is a very useful strategy that requires family members to keep ongoing records of the target behavior, and in some cases, correlates of the behavior. Among the many important functions, self-monitoring (1) provides a validity check of the nature, frequency, dura-

Table 4.1. (Continued)

9. Explore family relationships and interactions. Ask about:
   A. Relationship between parents.
   B. Parent–child interactions.
   C. Parents' expectations and family rules.
   D. Family decision making and child's involvement.
   E. Child's relationship with siblings and significant others.
10. Request information about the child's developmental history. Ask about:
   A. Pregnancy (e.g., complications, delivery).
   B. Infancy (e.g., temperament, developmental milestones).
   C. Toddler years (e.g., allergies, toilet training).
   D. Preschool years (e.g., preschool and kindergarten experiences and problems).
   E. Middle childhood (e.g., school entry, socialization experiences, problems).
   F. Early adolescence (e.g., physical maturity, difficulties with transitions).
11. Discuss the child's educational history. Ask about:
   A. Schools attended (including the number and location).
   B. Academic progress (e.g., grades, retentions, special education).
   C. Behavior and peer relationships at school.
12. Elicit information about the child's general health.
13. Explore the parents' consultation expectations.

[a] Only brief discussion of these items is necessary during the family interview. More extensive consideration of these issues is appropriate for the Conjoint Problem Identification Interview.
Source: Sanders, M. R., and Dadds, M. R. (1993). *Behavioral family intervention*. Boston: Allyn & Bacon. Reproduced with permission.

tion, and intensity of a problem; (2) allows for the collection of data for behaviors that are low in frequency, secretive, or nonobservable; (3) assesses the client's skills at tracking, labeling, and discriminating behaviors; (4) tests the client's adherence to treatment instructions prior to formal intervention; and (5) introduces family members to the idea that they are active participants

Table 4.2. Guidelines for Conducting a Child Interview

1. Set the child at ease with small talk.
2. Elicit the child's view of the reason for referral.
3. Establish the presenting complaint from the child's perspective:
   A. Ask the child to state what he or she sees as the main problem.
   B. If the child refuses to acknowledge a problem, ask him or her to describe a recent incident mentioned by the parents as problematic.
4. Clarify specific problem behaviors using active listening skills, elaboration, clarification, and requests for examples.
5. Explore associated problems by asking about other worries or concerns.
6. Request information on the child's social and friendship networks.

Source: Sanders, M. R., and Dadds, M. R. (1993). *Behavioral family intervention*. Boston: Allyn & Bacon. Reproduced with permission.

in the treatment process and that their perceptions are important (Sanders & Dadds, 1993).

When incorporating self-monitoring techniques into family assessments, consultants must be sure that the procedures are simple and that they generate meaningful and reliable data. The formats used for self-monitoring will provide the most reliable measures if they include clear directions and definitions of target behaviors (i.e., those behaviors to be recorded). Further, adherence to the self-monitoring procedures can be maximized by requesting that family members set aside times each day to record the behavior, or by scheduling them to coincide with naturally occurring events (e.g., after the children leave for school, immediately before or after meals, just before bedtime).

Self-report inventories completed by parents and children provide an additional method of family assessment. When using self-report inventories, consultants must keep in mind that such instruments produce results that are affected by a range of variables beyond the phenomena they seek to describe, including the respondent's personal and social adjustment, demand characteristics of the setting, and the child's developmental level. Therefore, it is always important to supplement self-reports with additional forms of assessment and informants. In general, measures can be collected regarding the child's general or specific behavioral characteristics, an individual parent's affective functioning, or the adjustment of an entire family. Detailed descriptions of self-report inventories are beyond the scope of this text; however, Table 4.3 provides a list of possible sources. For more information regarding family assessment scales, readers are referred to Grotevant and Carlson (1989). Information on measures of child dysfunction can be obtained from Impara and Murphy (1994).

Functional Analysis

The practice of behavioral consultation has expanded in recent years, both in terms of conceptual formats for the problem-solving process as well as of the assessment formats. Although a wide variety of assessment technologies can be used in consultation, the Problem Identification and Problem Analysis Interviews have served as the primary assessment technology to define the problem and analyze the functions of behavior. Many assessment techniques can be used to complement the problem-solving process and have been outlined in detail by Kratochwill and Sheridan (1990). In this section of the chapter, we also feature some recent advances that have been made in the

Table 4.3. Selected Self-Report Inventories

General Measures of Child Dysfunction

Child Behavior Checklist & Youth Self-Report Form (Achenbach, 1991a)
Teacher Rating Form (Achenbach, 1991b)
Revised Behavior Problem Checklist (Quay & Peterson, 1983)

Specific Measures of Child Dysfunction

Depression
    Child Depression Inventory (Kovacs, 1980)
    Reynolds Adolescent Depression Scale (W. Reynolds, 1986)
    Reynolds Child Depression Scale (W. Reynolds, 1989)
Hyperactivity
    Conners' Rating Scales (Conners, 1990)
Social Skills
    Social Skills Rating System (Gresham & Elliott, 1990)
    Walker-McConnell Scale of Social Competence (Walker & McConnell, 1988)
    School Social Behavior Scales (Merrell, 1993)
Anxiety
    Revised Children's Manifest Anxiety Scales (C. R. Reynolds & Richmond, 1985)
Fears
    Fear Survey Schedule for Children (Scherer & Nakamura, 1968)

Measures of Parental Dysfunction

Depression
    Beck Depression Inventory (Beck, Ward, Mendelson, Mock, & Erbaugh, 1961)
Anxiety
    State-Trait Anxiety Inventory (Spielberger, Gorsuch, & Lushene, 1970)
General Psychological Functioning
    General Health Questionnaire (Goldberg, 1972)
    Brief Symptom Inventory (Derogatis & Melisaratos, 1983)
Support
    Perceived Social Support Scales (Procidiano & Heller, 1983)
Risk for Abuse
    Child Abuse Potential Inventory (Milner, 1980)

Measures of Marital and Family Functioning

Family, Work, & Group Environment Scales (Moos, 1974)
Dyadic Adjustment Scale (Spanier, 1976)
Parenting Problems Checklist (Dadds & Powell, in press)
Parenting Stress Inventory (Abidin, 1983)
Family Adaptability and Cohesion Evaluation Scales III (FACES III) (Olson, Portner, & Lavee,
    1985)
Family Crisis Oriented Personal Scales (F-COPES) (McCubbin, Larsen, & Olson, 1982)

functional analysis of behavior and that can be integrated into the behavioral consultation problem-solving process.

Recent advances in the functional analysis of behavior have been made in terms both of defining problems and of relating the specific functions of behavior to a treatment technique. In this regard, conceptual advances have been made in the treatment validity of behavioral assessment tactics (see Hayes, Nelson, & Jarrett, 1986, 1987; Nelson, 1983). Several different defining characteristics of functional relationships have been outlined in the professional literature and can be considered by consultants in their problem-solving activities. The characteristics of functional relationships are outlined in Table 4.4. These characteristics have been defined by Haynes and O'Brien (1990). Given this conceptual framework for functional analysis, it is possible to specify some assessment methodologies that consultants can use in the problem-solving process.

Recently, information related to conducting a functional analysis has been conveyed by a number of writers (see especially the recent miniseries in the *Journal of Applied Behavior Analysis* edited by Neef & Iwata, 1994), building on the classic work of Iwata, Dorsey, Slifer, Bauman, and Richman (1982). Guidelines for how a functional analysis might be implemented have been provided and recently reviewed by Twernbold, Kratochwill, and Gardner (in press). One of the useful frameworks for a methodology of functional

---

Table 4.4. Characteristics of Functional Relationships

1. Functional relationships always imply covariance among variables; however, different types or forms of functional relationships exist (i.e., causal or correlational, controllable or uncontrollable, and important or trivial).
2. Functional relationships are probabilistic rather than exactly deterministic, due to the existence of unmeasured functional variables and measurement error.
3. Functional relationships are not exclusive; the existence of a functional relationship between a dependent variable and certain independent variables does not mean that other important functional relationships involving the dependent variable do not exist.
4. Functional relationships can vary over time and must be considered transient. The independent variables that are functionally related to a dependent variable, as well as the strength of the functional relationships, may change over time.
5. The role of the independent variable in a functional relationship varies and may be necessary, sufficient, necessary and sufficient, or neither necessary nor sufficient.
6. Functional relationships are conditional and have boundaries within which they operate.
7. Causal functional relationships can be reciprocal or bidirectional, and they require that the causal variable precede the event it causes.

Source: Haynes, S. N., and O'Brien, W. H. (1990). Functional analysis in behavior therapy. *Clinical Psychology Review, 10*, 649-668. Reproduced with permission.

Interview the person and those who know him/her best

Direct observation over an extended time period

Systematic manipulations

Figure 4.1. Three stages that can be used to collect information for a functional analysis. (*Source*: Adapted from O'Neill, R. E., Horner, R. H., Albin, R. W., Storey, K., & Sprague, J. R. [1990]. *Functional analysis of problem behavior: A practical assessment guide.* Pacific Grove, CA: Brooks/Cole. Reproduced with permission.)

analysis was presented by O'Neill, Horner, Albin, Storey, and Sprague (1990). Figure 4.1 provides an overview of their model. Specifically, these authors indicate that a functional analysis must include a description of the undesirable behavior couched in operational terms, a prediction of the times and situations when a behavior will or will not be performed across various routines (e.g., classroom routine), and a definition of functions such as maintaining reinforcers that the undesirable behaviors produce for the child. The Functional Analysis Interview (O'Neill et al., 1990) investigates a range of variables that influence problematic behavior, many of which have been integrated into the Conjoint Problem Identification Interview. In addition, O'Neill et al. (1990) recommend an observational format and have developed a Functional Analysis Observation Form that can assist in the direct observation of behavior and allow gathering of information on behavior, setting events, discriminative stimuli, functions, and actual consequence of behavior. The final phase of their approach involves direct manipulation of variables to examine the responsiveness of various problematic behaviors to the manipulated features. This experimental paradigm allows one to test hypotheses through observation of actual behavior change.

Several other approaches to the organization of the assessment methodology for functional analysis have been presented, including that by Mace, Lalli, and Pinter-Lalli (1991). Figure 4.2 provides the methodology these authors have used to conduct the functional analytical strategy and is reviewed in greater detail below. In the first assessment format, called "descrip-

```
┌─────────────────────────────────────────────────────────────┐
│                                                               │
│            Descriptive Analysis of Natural Conditions         │
│                                                               │
│                                                               │
│            Hypothesis of Functional Relationships             │
│                                                               │
│                                                               │
│            Experimental Analysis under Analogue Conditions    │
│                                                               │
│                                                               │
│      Intervention Development, Implementation, and Evaluation │
│                                                               │
│                                                               │
│       Maintenance and Generalization of Intervention Effects  │
│                                                               │
│                                                               │
└─────────────────────────────────────────────────────────────┘
```

Figure 4.2. Comprehensive functional analysis methodology. (*Source*: Adapted from Mace, F. C., Lalli, J. S., & Pinter-Lalli, E. [1991]. Functional analysis and treatment of aberrant behavior. *Research in Developmental Disabilities*, *12*, 155–180. Reproduced with permission.)

tive analysis," the consultant does not have control over environmental conditions but rather describes behaviors in terms of their antecedent, sequential, and consequent functions. In this format, the Conjoint Problem Identification Interview can be used and supplemented with direct observation. Such a strategy incorporates procedures that follow a basic antecedent behavior and consequent recording function. These procedures are based on the work of Bijou and his associates for descriptive behavioral assessment (e.g., Bijou, Peterson, & Ault, 1968; Bijou, Peterson, Harris, Allen, & Johnson, 1969). In addition to procedures developed by Bijou and his associates, a variety of descriptive procedures that incorporate questionnaires, checklists, and rating scales can be used. The Motivational Assessment Scale developed by Durand and Crimmins (1988) consists of a 16-item questionnaire designed to generate information and evaluate hypotheses pertaining to functions of behavior. The Problem Behavior Questionnaire (Lewis, Scott, & Suguai, in press) is a 15-item scale that assesses behavior problems in relation to three response classes: (1) behaviors that function to gain peer or teacher attention, (2) behaviors that function to avoid peer or teacher attention, and (3) setting events.

In addition to descriptive procedures, the phase outlined by Mace and his associates incorporates hypothesized functional relationships. Such hypothesized functions can occur following the Conjoint Problem Identification Interview and other supplementary descriptive analyses. Descriptive data may provide important hypotheses regarding variables that maintain problematic child, teacher, or parent behavior. A major concern with this descriptive analysis is that such information may not correspond to experimentally manipulated data in either analogue or naturalistic settings.

Analogue experimental assessment can be used by directly manipulating various environmental conditions and analyzing antecedent and consequent conditions that are hypothesized to control behavior in more naturalistic settings such as classroom or community environments. One of the major issues that analogue procedures are designed to overcome is the rather costly time-consuming process that often occurs in manipulating naturalistic contingencies. Some analogue assessment procedures have been developed that can be implemented in a relatively brief period of time (e.g., 90 minutes). Work by Wacker and his associates (e.g., L. J. Cooper, Wacker, Sasso, Reimers, & Donn, 1990; Harding, Wacker, Cooper, Millard, & Jensen-Kovalan, 1994; Wacker et al., 1994) illustrates this process. For example, Harding et al. (1994) used parents to conduct assessments in their outpatient clinic. Prior to the assessment, the parents were given a hierarchy of antecedent and consequent components for their children's problem behavior. The children were experiencing a variety of inappropriate conduct problems and met DSM-III-R diagnostic criteria for conduct disorder. The authors conducted an assessment of potential treatment components to identify the variables that were presumed to control the children's behavior. They found that in a relatively brief session the behavior of six of the seven children could be improved with the various treatment procedures implemented. These kinds of brief functional analytical techniques have allowed the application of functional assessment with many clients in a very short period of time and could be used to supplement the consultation model.

A major feature of the analogue assessment technique is that it allows tight control over treatment procedures and environmental contingencies. In addition, parents can often be trained to a criterion to effectively carry out the procedure. Such procedures have also been used with teachers in applied settings. The disadvantages of the analogue technique are that it may be difficult to sample some problem behaviors such as those with low-frequency occurrence or that there might be some difficulties in matching analogue conditions to those that exist in the natural setting. Since functional assessment is often a matter of context (see Carr, 1994), some of the context variables in naturalistic settings may not be matched in analogue functional assessment.

Another option involves combining various assessment procedures and developing a consensual validation for the various functions of behavior. In this regard, both descriptive and experimental techniques might be used. For example, Sasso et al. (1992) trained classroom teachers to conduct descriptive functional analysis and an experimental functional analysis for children who were experiencing autism. The authors found that in both assessment methods, negative reinforcement was identified as a maintaining variable for the students' behavior. In this regard, combined assessment techniques allowed the design of an intervention program that effectively changed the problematic behaviors of these students.

A major consideration when thinking about combining various functional analytical assessment strategies is that functional assessment should be conceptualized as a *process* ongoing throughout the consultation process. When functional assessment is considered an ongoing process rather than a one-time event, more valuable information for the design of instructional and behavioral programs could likely be obtained (Horner, 1994). That is, the consultant might make use of ongoing functional assessment information from teachers, parents, and other care providers throughout the consultation process. Eventually, directly manipulated tests during the treatment implementation phase of consultation would be most useful.

In summary, functional analytical strategies have been recently promoted as a major development within the applied behavior analysis field. Development of functional analysis is important in conjoint consultation inasmuch as parents and teachers may identify very different functions of behavior across settings. That is, treatment programs may need to be tailor-made for each setting depending on the context, setting events, and other features of maintaining consequences of behavior across various settings. The complexity of this assessment process need not overshadow the time-efficient features of consultation. An important guiding principle driving functional assessment is the high probability that identifying functions of behavior will increase treatment validity, thereby allowing the consultant to actually spend less time retuning and cycling back through the consultation problem-solving process. Recent advances in functional assessment have great potential to add to the tools and technology of consultants conducting consultation in applied settings.

Conjoint Problem Identification Interview

The Conjoint Problem Identification Interview (CPII) provides a format for guiding consultees through the steps of problem identification. In Chapter 1, various objectives of the problem identification stage (and PIIs) were presented. These same objectives are relevant in conjoint behavioral consultation; however, the establishment of the parent–teacher relationship is also important. The six goals of problem identification in conjoint behavioral consultation are to:

1	Establish a positive working relationship between parents and teacher, and between the consultant and consultees.
2	Define the problem(s) in operational terms.
3	Provide a tentative identification of behavior(s) in terms of antecedent, situation, and consequent conditions across settings.
4	Provide a tentative strength of the behavior across settings (e.g., how often or severe).
5	Discuss and reach agreement on a goal for behavior change across settings.
6	Establish a procedure for collection of baseline or pretest data across settings in terms of sampling plan, what data are to be collected, who is to collect the data, and how the behavior is to be recorded.

It is recommended that the consultant actively direct the interview to allow equal input from both parties. Through careful discussion, strategic questioning, and consultant guidance, pertinent information can be elicited from both parties in a focused, systematic fashion. One practical way to increase participation is to present open-ended questions, encourage verbal exchanges between parent and teacher, validate statements made by both parties, and explore and highlight behavioral similarities and differences across settings. This discussion will provide opportunities for parent and teacher to discuss issues and observations with the consultant and with each other, and can be followed up with direct questions when necessary. Throughout this discussion, the consultant should encourage consultees to work together as partners, rather than in a separate or parallel manner. Definitions and examples of each interview objective are presented in Table 4.5. Recommendations for conducting CPIIs are provided in Table 4.6. A structured CPII form for behavioral parent–teacher consultation is presented in the Appendix.

Perhaps one of the major difficulties in problem identification is the operational definition of the problem. Although it is essential that a target behavior be articulated in concrete and specific terms, doing so may require several data collection and analysis sessions. As emphasized earlier, it may be useful to consider this early stage of consultation as a process. The outcome of early problem-identification efforts might be a tentative delineation of a behavioral focus. As data continue to be collected, hypotheses regarding the function of behaviors will continue to be formulated and tested. Thus, the

Table 4.5. Conjoint Problem Identification Interview Objectives, Definitions, and Examples

Objective	Definition	Examples
Opening Salutation	General opening statement.	"Hello! Thanks for coming in today."
General Statement to Open Consultation	General statement to begin discussion related to referral concerns.	"What seems to be the problem?" "What is it that you are concerned about?"
Behavior Specification	Behavioral descriptions of client functioning are elicited, with a focus on *specific* behaviors. Several examples of the general problem are requested. Whenever possible, a problem that occurs across settings should be targeted.	
	Behavioral description	"What does Jamie do when he's 'angry?'" "Tell me what you mean when you say he 'gets upset with himself easily.'" "Give me some examples of what you mean by 'self-abusive' behaviors."
	Elicit examples	"What are some more examples of Jamie's 'self-abusive' behaviors at home/at school?"
	Prioritize behavior	"We've discussed several behaviors, such as hitting himself, kicking objects, ripping up papers, and screaming. Which of these is most problematic across settings?" "Do you both agree?"
Target Behavior Definition	Specific operational definition of target behavior. An operational definition is one that is objective, concrete, and observable.	"Let's define exactly what we mean by Jamie hitting himself...he raises his arm, clenches his fist, and slaps the side of his head with force...is that right?"
History of Problem	An estimate of the duration of the problem behavior, including how long it has been occurring, any changes in its topography or frequency, or other unique characteristics.	"How long has this behavior been a problem?" "Has the behavior always presented itself this way, or has it changed over time?"

Behavior Setting	A precise description of the settings in which the target problem behavior occurs. Ask for as many examples of settings at home and at school as possible. Prioritize the settings from the most to the least severe.	
	General setting description	"Where is Jamie usually when he hits himself?" "Give me some examples of where Jamie does this at school." "Where does the head-slapping occur at home?"
	Elicit examples	"What are some more examples of where this occurs?"
	Prioritize setting	"Which of the settings at school is most problematic?" "Which of the settings at home is most problematic?"
Conditional/Functional Analysis		
Antecedent Conditions and Setting Events	Events or variables that precede the child's behavior. These events can immediately precede the behavior, or they may be removed in time (e.g., events at home in the morning that affect the child's behaviors at school).	"What typically happens at home/at school before Jamie starts to hit himself?" "What things do you notice before he starts that might be contributing to its occurrence?" "What is a typical morning like before Jamie goes to school?"
Consequent Conditions	Events that occur immediately following the behavior. These can be environmental in nature, or reactions/responses of parents, teachers, or peers. They can occur immediately following the behavior or at a later point in time (e.g., at home after school).	"What typically happens after Jamie hits himself at home/at school?" "How do others react when Jamie slaps his head?" "What types of things do you notice at home/at school after Jamie hits himself that might be affecting its occurrence?" "How are school-related problems handled at home?"

(Continued)

Table 4.5. (Continued)

Environmental/Sequential Conditions	Situational events or environmental conditions occurring when the behavior occurs. A pattern or trend of antecedent/consequent conditions across a series of occasions (e.g. time of day, day of week). This may include activities, persons, situations, or other variables that appear to be related to the target behavior.	"What else is typically happening when Jamie hits himself?" "What patterns do you notice in Jamie's head-slapping behavior?" "What time of day or day of week seems to be most problematic at home/at school?" "Who else is usually present?" "Is the head slapping more frequent in some situations than in others?"
Behavior Strength across Settings	The level or incidence of the behavior. The most common features concern how often (frequent) or how long (duration) the behavior occurs. The question format (i.e., whether to ask about frequency, duration, latency, intensity) will depend on the specific behavior and focus of consultation.	"How often does Jamie hit himself at home/at school?" "How long does it last?"
Goal of Consultation	Appropriate or acceptable level of the behavior. Both long- and short-term goals should be discussed.	"What would be an acceptable level of head-slapping at home/at school?" "Is any hitting OK?" "What would you like to see for Jamie?" "Is there general agreement on our goal for Jamie across home and school?"
Existing Procedures	Procedures or programs/rules in force that are external to the child and to the behavior.	"What are some programs or procedures that are currently operating in the classroom/at home?" "How is the problem currently dealt with at home/school?"
Child's Strengths/Assets	Strengths, abilities, or other positive features of the child.	"What are some of the things that Jamie is good at?" "What are some of Jamie's strengths?"
Possible Reinforcers	Social, concrete, or activity-based reinforcers that may be used in a behavioral program.	"What are some things (e.g. events, activities) that Jamie finds reinforcing?" "What are some things Jamie likes to do?"

Rationale for Data Collection	A purpose or rationale for data collection.	"It would be very helpful to watch Jamie for a week or so and monitor how often he hits himself in the head. This will help us key in on some important facts that we may have missed, and also help us document the progress that Jamie makes."
Cross-Setting Data Collection Procedures	Procedural details regarding data recording, including the kind of measure, what is to be recorded, and how to record. Specific details of data recording should be provided. Consistent data collection procedures across settings should be encouraged. A written plan for parents and teachers is often helpful.	"What would be a simple way for you to keep track of the number of times Jamie hits his head at home/at school?" "We've decided that at home, you will keep a count of the number of times Jamie hits his head each evening, including the time and preceding events. At school, you will chart the number of times Jamie hits himself, as well as what happens before and after, and who is present and how they respond."
Date to Begin Data Collection	Procedural details regarding when to begin collecting data.	"When can you begin to collect data at home/at school?" "Can you both start the recording procedures tomorrow?"
Next Appointment	Meeting time for CPAI.	"When can we all get together again to discuss the data and determine where to go from here?"
Closing Salutation	General statement closing the interview.	"Thanks for your time and hard work! See you soon!"

Table 4.6. Suggestions for Conducting Problem Identification Interviews in Conjoint Behavioral Consultation

1. Begin the interview by eliciting general concerns from the parents and teacher. Ask for specific examples of each general concern as it occurs at home and school.
2. Summarize the general concerns and examples across settings. Try to point out similarities from the parent's and the teacher's examples.
3. Explain that not all problems can be addressed at once. Ask the parents' and teacher what they consider a priority. This priority can be determined by selecting the behavior that is of greatest concern or one that can affect other behaviors if targeted. Gain consensus from all consultees.
4. Define the priority (i.e., target behavior) clearly and objectively. The definition should be observable and concrete.
5. Keep the discussion focused by restating the target problem and summarizing often. Ask both the parents and the teacher for validation to ensure agreement and understanding at both home and school.
6. Ask about antecedents and consequences to the target problem at both home and school. Inquire about any patterns that parents and teachers may see in its occurrence. This information may include day of week, time of day, and other commonalities across instances.
7. Determine both short-term objectives and long-term goals for the student at home and at school. The objectives should be appropriate for the setting (i.e., home and school), based on opportunities and severity. An example of a short-term objective is: "Kevin will wait his turn and ask to join in ongoing games with a clear and pleasant voice at least 3 times during each lunch recess [school] and once a day when playing with his brother [home]."
8. Develop data collection procedures that are simple and practical. Whenever possible, use similar data collection procedures at home and school to allow for direct comparisons. Be sure that the consultees help develop these procedures and that they state whether they will be able to follow through with the collection procedures. Determine the length of baseline data collection.
9. Collect additional data that may be helpful in identifying and understanding the problem, such as work samples, rating scales, self-reports, and sociometric measures.
10. Check in with the parents and teacher midway through the baseline period to monitor adherence to the data collection procedures.

problem identification/problem analysis process involves a continued refinement of target behaviors that encompass child, parent, teacher, and environmental variables.

STAGE 2: PROBLEM ANALYSIS

During the problem analysis stage of conjoint behavioral consultation, the consultant and consultees use the available behavioral information, including that derived from functional analysis, to design a plan to achieve problem solution across settings. The consultant's role is to (1) assist consultees to identify variables across settings that might influence the attainment of problem solution and (2) help develop a meaningful, effective plan that will be consistent (i.e., compatible) across settings. The consultees' roles are to clarify behavioral data and assist in the generation and selection of a plan and plan tactics.

Several variables can be highlighted during problem analysis, including cross-setting antecedents, situations during which the behavior does not occur, and consequences operating to maintain behaviors. Environmental variables operating regularly within the home and school settings must be identified and analyzed. Particular emphasis should be placed on the identification of *setting events* (Wahler & Fox, 1981). Setting events are environmental variables that are temporally or contextually removed from the target behavior, but are nevertheless related to its occurrence. For example, early-morning child–parent interactions or events in the home setting (such as arguments, temper tantrums, an unhealthy breakfast) may serve as setting events to child behaviors manifested later at school. Although temporally and contextually removed from the school setting, these events may be clearly related to the occurrence of the target behavior at school. Likewise, events at school (such as a playground fight, verbal reprimands by the teacher, poor grades) may trigger certain behavioral patterns at home. Given the reciprocal nature of the home–school interface, setting events are particularly relevant in conjoint consultation. Because persons across settings are involved simultaneously throughout problem identification and analysis, delineation of ecological conditions and setting events may be particularly feasible within the context of conjoint problem solving.

Attitudes and expectations of significant others (parents, teachers, siblings, peers) within and between settings, as well as daily classroom, school, and home routines, can be explored. Finally, because parents and teachers are working collaboratively, all resources that potentially may be used in the development and implementation of a comprehensive treatment plan can be identified. Again, the parameters of the intervention should not be limited solely to child behaviors. Because the scope and focus of the target are broadened, interventions may occur at several levels (e.g., home–school communication, manipulation of setting events, environmental restructuring). And, because the child exists in overlapping ecological systems, changes in one system can influence other systems.

Treatment Acceptability

An important consideration in plan development is that of treatment acceptability. As discussed in Chapter 1, *treatment acceptability* has to do with the perceptions of consultees regarding intervention procedures. Interventions that are high in cost (in terms of time, effort, or resources) are likely to be implemented sporadically, partially, or not at all. Furthermore, those that run counter to the orientation or philosophy of the consultees may not be adopted. Interventions that are positive in nature tend to be perceived more favorably to consultees than those with negative or aversive components. Consultees also tend to perceive any intervention more favorably for severe problems compared to interventions for nonserious difficulties (Witt et al., 1984).

The notion of treatment acceptability has specific importance in conjoint behavioral consultation. Consistency in programming across home and school settings is a primary objective; therefore, the intervention developed with parents and teachers must be viewed as acceptable and reasonable to both parties, and not simply to one teacher or one parent. This is not to say that identical procedures must be implemented at both home and school (in fact, outcomes of a functional analysis may contraindicate doing so); however, it is necessary that the program be complementary and supported across settings. Personal and interpersonal dynamics may affect the degree to which parents, teachers, and the consultant can agree on a general strategy and specific plan tactics. The importance of building a strong and positive relationship between parents and teachers is highlighted in this phase of consultation.

A related issue in problem analysis and plan development concerns consultees' attitudes and perceptions about behavioral strategies. For example, an intervention requiring a parent to provide positive reinforcement to her son for completing his homework might be deemed unacceptable if the mother perceives this practice as "bribery." Some teachers might report that they "don't believe in" giving an individual student stars or tokens for engaging in behaviors or completing tasks that are required of the entire class. In these cases, it is important that the consultant use good interpersonal skills to educate consultees about the documented effectiveness of such procedures and the importance of individualizing treatment plans to address a student's needs. At the same time, however, the consultant should attempt to maintain the stance of a collaborative partner in the relationship. Nevertheless, it is the consultant's responsibility to see that appropriate services are delivered to the student, and the consultant can use a combination of behavioral expertise and positive interpersonal skills to maximize consultation outcomes. A number of interpersonal influence strategies that may be considered by consultants are described in Cialdini (1993).

───────────────────────────────── Conjoint Problem Analysis Interview

The Conjoint Problem Analysis Interview (CPAI) provides an opportunity to explore cross-setting conditions surrounding the problem and discuss all of the procedural details of the intervention. As with the CPII, strategic interviewing skills on the part of the consultant should maximize equal participation and shared ownership of the intervention.

The objectives of problem analysis (and PAIs) were presented in Chapter 1. These same objectives are important in conjoint behavioral consultations; however, more information will be available to the consultant and consultees. The identification of setting events to aid in the functional analysis of problems is particularly relevant in the CPAI during conjoint consultation. Specific goals for this stage include:

1	Evaluate and obtain agreement on the sufficiency and adequacy of baseline data across settings.
2	Conduct a tentative functional analysis of the behavior across settings (i.e., discuss antecedent, consequent, and sequential conditions).
3	Identify setting events (events that are functionally related, but temporally or contextually distal to the target behavior), ecological conditions, and other cross-setting variables that may impact the target behaviors across settings.
4	Design a cross-setting intervention plan including specification of conditions to be changed and the practical guidelines regarding treatment implementation.
5	Reaffirm record-keeping procedures across settings.

Operational definitions and examples of the CPAI objectives are included in Table 4.7. Additional suggestions for conducting PAIs in conjoint behavioral consultation are presented in Table 4.8. A structured CPAI form is presented in the Appendix.

───────────────────────── STAGE 3: TREATMENT (PLAN) IMPLEMENTATION

Stage III of conjoint behavioral consultation involves the implementation of the treatment strategy agreed upon during the problem analysis stage. The

Table 4.7. Conjoint Problem Analysis Interview Objectives, Definitions, and Examples

Objective	Definition	Examples
Opening Salutation	General opening statement.	"Hello! How are you both today?"
General Statement Regarding Data and Problem	General statement to begin discussion related to target problem and baseline data.	"Were you able to keep a record of the number of times Jamie hit himself on the head this week?"
Behavior Strength across Settings	Question or statement regarding target behavior, specific to the data being collected.	"According to the data, it looks like Jamie hit himself in the head at least 4 times at home and 5 times at school each day." "It happened most frequently on Monday, and he was with three or more persons when it happened."
Antecedent Conditions	Information regarding events that precede the child's behavior. These events may have immediately preceded the behavior, or they may have been removed in time (e.g., events at home in the morning that impact the child's behaviors at school). Refer to specific instances documented in the baseline data in this discussion.	"What did you notice before Jamie began to hit himself at home/at school?" "What things may have led up to its occurrence?" "What happened in the morning before Jamie went to school on those high-frequency days?"
Consequent Conditions	Events that occurred following the behavior. These can be reactions of parents, teachers, or peers, and they can occur immediately following the behavior or at a later point in time (e.g., at home after school). Refer to specific instances documented in the baseline data in this discussion.	"What happened after Jamie hit himself at home/at school?" "What types of things did you notice afterward that may have maintained its occurrence?" "How did the other persons respond?"

Sequential Conditions	Situational events or environmental conditions occurring when the behavior occurs. A pattern or trend of antecedent/consequent conditions across a series of occasions (e.g., time of day, day of week).	"What else was happening in the classroom/playground/home when you observed Jamie hitting himself?" "What was Jamie doing when he began slapping himself?" "What time of day or day of week seemed most problematic?" "What was different about Monday that might have increased the frequency?" "What patterns did you notice in Jamie's behavior at home/at school?"
Behavior Interpretation	Parents' and teachers' perceptions regarding the purpose or function of the behavior. Consultant may also suggest hypotheses regarding the behavior if other explanations are plausible. Hypotheses should be environmental/behavioral in nature and should lead to the development of a meaningful intervention.	"Why do you think Jamie hits himself?" "It sounds like it might also be related to a very low frustration tolerance level or changes in routine."
Cross-Setting Plan Development	An intervention to be implemented across settings. Specific strategies should be delineated. The tentative goal stated in the CPII, the interpretation (function) of the behavior, and the child's strengths should be considered in the plan.	"It seems that we need to try something different." "What can be done at both home and school to stop Jamie from hitting himself and to teach him alternative, more appropriate ways to cope with frustration?"
Data Recording Procedures	Data recording procedures to be used in treatment implementation. Data collected should be identical to or consistent with baseline data collection procedures (i.e., specified in CPII).	"It would be very helpful if we could continue to collect data on the number of times that Jamie hits himself each day at home and school." "Can we continue the same recording procedures as before?"
Next Appointment	Meeting time for the CTEI.	"When can we get together in the next two weeks to discuss how things are going with the plan?"
Closing Salutation	General statement to close interview.	"Thanks for your hard work! See you soon!"

Table 4.8. Suggestions for Conducting Problem Analysis Interviews in Conjoint Behavioral Consultation

1. Start the interview by asking the parents and teacher how the data collection went. Review the data in the presence of the consultees.
2. Use the behavioral data to structure your questions. Ask about specific instances of the behavior, including what happened before, during, and after its occurrence.
3. Ask about setting events, such as events at home that occurred in conjunction with the target behavior at school, or happenings at school and how they relate to behaviors at school.
4. Try to point out any interesting patterns or trends that are apparent in the data. Highlight similarities, differences, and relationships between the home and school settings if they become apparent.
5. Summarize the data that were collected at home and school and ask whether the problem still warrants intervention across settings.
6. On the basis of the data that were collected and the observations of consultees, inquire about what may be maintaining or reinforcing the problem behavior at home and school. Restate any internal or psychological causes in behavioral or environmental terms.
7. Using the information gleaned from the data analysis and the hypotheses about what promotes or maintains the problem behavior, develop an intervention plan. Use information available regarding empirically validated interventions to select treatment strategies.
8. Involve the consultees as much as possible in the development of the plan. Ask what is reasonable and practical in their setting. Ask for their input about the length of the program and the reinforcers to be used. If feasible, include a home-school communication mechanism, such as a home-note procedure.
9. Suggest that similar programs be implemented in both the home and school settings to increase consistency in the program and maintenance of the behavior change.
10. Ask consultees to continue collecting behavioral data during treatment implementation. Data collection procedures should be identical to those used during the problem identification (baseline) stage.

expanded (i.e., cross-setting) behavioral intervention base is desirable to promote consistency across settings (Kratochwill & Sheridan, 1990). During treatment implementation, the possibility of behavioral *side effects* (undesired intervention effects that are unplanned or unexpected) and *contrast effects* (effects in nontreatment settings or conditions that run counter to those under treatment conditions) should also be assessed. The assessment of such effects can be readily made, since individuals from various settings are involved in conjoint consultation. Modifications in the program can be made immediately if such effects are observed. Furthermore, cross-setting interventions should enhance generalization of treatment effects.

Certain intervention components have been identified that may increase the effectiveness of programs. For example, an acceptable cost–return ratio, minimal intrusion in terms of time and facilities, and ease in implementation have been identified as important in home–school programs (Nye, 1989). Complicated and costly intervention plans are likely to be perceived as unacceptable to consultees and may be implemented incorrectly, sporadically, or not at all.

Treatment integrity is an additional consideration that can affect outcomes of consultation interventions. *Treatment integrity* is defined as the degree to which intervention plans are implemented as designed or intended (or with "fidelity"). With the added complexities of cross-setting interventions and multiple treatment agents, adherence to treatment components across home and school is especially important. Procedures to increase treatment integrity include (1) providing consultees with specific written information regarding plan tactics and responsibilities; (2) training consultees in intervention components through modeling, rehearsal, and feedback; (3) conducting direct observations and providing feedback regarding intervention implementation; (4) arranging booster sessions with consultees to meet periodically and discuss intervention components; and (5) requesting that consultees self-monitor (i.e., provide a record of) their own behaviors related to completing the important intervention procedures. Additional considerations and strategies to increase treatment integrity can be found in Gresham (1989).

It is critical to continue the data collection process during treatment implementation. To ensure comparability between baseline and intervention data, identical observation procedures should be used. These observation procedures should be simple and straightforward to enhance consultees' willingness and ability to collect data reliably. Existing data in the form of records, logs, assignments, and other products are useful if the problem definition warrants such measures.

Table 4.9 identifies various consultant practices to be initiated during the treatment-implementation stage of conjoint behavioral consultation. Perhaps most important is the need for consultants to be available to answer questions, address concerns, and support consultees.

STAGE 4: TREATMENT (PLAN) EVALUATION

The purpose of treatment evaluation is to determine the attainment of consultation goals and the efficacy of the treatment across settings. The data provided through formal treatment evaluation allow the parents, teachers, and consultant to determine further action. Depending on the initial outcomes of the intervention, the consultant and consultees may decide to (1) continue the existing program to strengthen treatment effects, (2) modify one or more

Table 4.9. Consultant Practices during the Treatment Implementation Stage

1. Check with consultees on the first scheduled day of the intervention to ensure that they have the necessary information and materials to proceed.
2. Schedule a time to observe the consultees implementing some intervention components. To minimize resistance, ensure the consultees that the purpose of the observation is support and assistance, not evaluation of their skills.
3. Provide consultees with feedback regarding your observations. Frame the feedback in supportive, facilitative terms.
4. Demonstrate intervention procedures if necessary. In some cases, the consultant may be the primary intervention agent initially (and very briefly) as a model for the consultee. If this training approach is used, fade the consultant's involvement as soon as possible.
5. Check in periodically with the consultees to ensure that the intervention procedures are progressing as planned and that the data collection continues. Schedule frequent phone calls with parents to ensure that they are supported throughout this consultation stage.
6. Ask consultees for subjective evaluations of how the program is working. If possible, ask to see some preliminary data. If no progress is being made after several days (or if there is behavioral regression), schedule a brief meeting with the parents and teacher to discuss some immediate plan modifications.
7. Confirm the date, time, and location for a formal evaluation of the intervention via the Conjoint Treatment Evaluation Interview.

treatment components to enhance plan effectiveness, (3) change treatment strategies entirely, (4) withdraw the intervention gradually or completely, or (5) recycle through problem identification or analysis to reassess the appropriateness of the target definition or the accuracy of hypotheses surrounding the functional analysis. The majority of cases, warrant some modification and continuation of the intervention plan.

Conjoint Treatment Evaluation Interview

The Conjoint Treatment Evaluation Interview (CTEI) helps the consultant structure the process of data analysis and determine the future of the consultation relationship (continuation, termination, or planning for maintenance and follow-up). In Chapter 1, the specific objectives of treatment evaluation (and TEIs) were presented. These objectives are similar for conjoint behavioral consultation, with particular attention paid to cross-setting treatment effectiveness and maintenance of the parent–teacher relationship. The four goals of treatment evaluation in conjoint behavioral consultation are to:

1   Determine whether the goals of consultation have been attained across settings.

2	Evaluate the effectiveness of the treatment plan across settings.
3	Discuss strategies and tactics regarding the continuation, modification, or termination of the treatment plan.
4	Schedule additional interviews, if necessary, or terminate consultation.

Interview objectives, definitions, and examples are presented in Table 4.10. Suggestions for implementing CTEIs are in Table 4.11. A structured CTEI form is presented in the Appendix.

To measure maintenance of the treatment effects gleaned through conjoint consultation, systematic methods of consultee and client follow-up are necessary. This follow-up includes assessment of child behavior change, consultee skills, and the parent–teacher relationship. Direct and indirect assessments (e.g., behavioral observations, interviews, and checklists or rating scales) may be used to assess all of these areas objectively. In the case where behavioral or skill regression occurs, further problem analysis, treatment programming, or consultee training may be appropriate.

Depending on several case-related factors (e.g., parent and teacher variables, severity of the problem, recurrence or nonrecurrence of target behaviors), consultees may or may not have continued to engage in collaborative interactions. Methods to reestablish open communication and parent–teacher partnerships should be implemented. For example, home–school notes, regular telephone contacts, or the establishment of a structured parent-involvement program (such as periodic meetings, volunteering in the classroom, or enrichment activities at home) might be considered.

DISCUSSION QUESTIONS

1	How can functional analysis procedures be incorporated systematically into conjoint behavioral consultation?
2	What are some possible targets in conjoint behavioral consultation that relate to parent–teacher communication or home–school relationship issues?
3	Provide several examples of setting events that might contribute to the occurrence of target behaviors at school and at home.
4	What are some difficulties that a consultant may encounter when developing an intervention plan?

Table 4.10. Conjoint Treatment Evaluation Interview Objectives, Definitions, and Examples

Objective	Definition	Examples
Opening Salutation	General opening statement.	"Hello again!"
General Procedures	Question or statement regarding general procedures and outcome.	"How did things go with the plan?"
Goal Attainment across Settings	Determines specifically if the goals of consultation have been attained at home and school. Refer to treatment data collected and the goal statement specified in the CPII.	"Has our goal of one or less 'head slap' per day been met at home/at school?"
Plan Modifications	New plan strategies to increase plan effectiveness across settings. Consultant may suggest a change or question the need for change. If plan is successful and goals are met, this question may be inapplicable.	"How can we modify the procedures so that the plan is more effective at home/at school?"
Plan Effectiveness across Settings	Determines the effectiveness of the specific plan at home and school for the specific child (i.e., the internal validity of the plan). Identifies other possible competing explanations. If consultation goals have not been met, this question may be inapplicable.	"Do you think that the behavior program was responsible for Jamie's decrease in head-slapping?" "Were there any other things happening that might have caused a temporary change?"
External Validity of Plan	Determines the potential effectiveness of the plan for another child who has a similar problem. Doing so may also increase the potential for consultees to generalize the plan to other clients. If consultation goals have not been met, this question may be inapplicable.	"Do you think this plan would work with another child with similar difficulties?"

Postimplementation Planning	Decision regarding the advisability of leaving the plan in effect, removing the plan, or constructing a new plan. Selecting a posttreatment alternative to implement across settings may occur. If consultation goals have not been met, this question may be inapplicable.	"Should we leave the plan in effect for a while longer?"
Procedures for Generalization/Maintenance	Procedures to encourage continued progress across settings. The goal is to encourage generalization to other behaviors, persons, or situations, or to maintain behavior over a long period of time. If the goals of consultation are not met, this question may be inapplicable.	"How can we encourage Jamie to display these behavior changes in other problem settings?" "What *procedures* should we use to make sure that the behavior change continues over time?"
Follow-up Assessment Procedures	Follow-up recording procedures to monitor the behavior over time and over settings. If consultation goals have not been met, this question may be inapplicable.	"How can we monitor Jamie's progress to ensure that these positive changes continue?"
Need for Future Interviews/Next Appointment	Question or statement to assess need for additional interviews or meetings.	"When can we meet again to discuss the effectiveness of our modified plan?" "Would you like to meet again to check on Jamie's progress?"
Termination of Consultation	Question or statement to end consultation interactions if goals have been met.	"It seems as though we are finished with our formal consultation meetings."
Closing Salutation	General statement to close interview.	"Thanks for everything! Good-bye!"

Table 4.11. Suggestions for Conducting Treatment Evaluation Interviews in Conjoint Behavioral Consultation

1. Begin the interview by reviewing the data collected by parents and teachers during the plan implementation stage. Review the data in the presence of the consultees.
2. Compare the occurrence of the behavior at home and school. Compare the frequency or severity of the target problem during treatment to baseline.
3. Solicit the parents' and teacher's perceptions about the effectiveness of the intervention at home and school. Review the behavioral goals established for each setting during the CPII. Ask how consultees feel about the student's responsiveness to treatment.
4. Ask consultees for their preference about what to do next. In general, consultation procedures can be continued or terminated, and treatment plans can be maintained, modified, or faded.
5. If consultation goals have been met and the treatment will be faded, recommend that it be done gradually to increase maintenance.
6. If some progress is seen but modifications are necessary to increase the student's performance, try small changes first.
7. If no progress is seen, recycle through problem analysis and try to determine other conditions that may be maintaining the unacceptable behavior. It may also be necessary to question the adequacy of the problem definition; it may be that the "wrong" problem was selected.
8. In some cases, treatment effects will be seen in one setting and not the other. It may be necessary to make individualized (setting-specific) decisions about the future of the treatment plan based on the student's responsiveness to the program at home and school. Regardless of whether a program is continued across both settings, both the parents and the teacher should continue to be involved as consultees.
9. Reinforce consultees for their hard work in implementing the intervention, regardless of the outcome!
10. Set up future meeting times to review the student's performance.
11. Encourage parents and teachers to continue communicating and collaborating on the student's behalf.

| 5 | What are some unique issues during treatment implementation in conjoint behavioral consultation, as compared to teacher-only or parent-only consultation? |
| 6 | What are some possible outcomes determined during treatment evaluation? What factors are important to consider when determining the "next step" in a conjoint behavioral consultation case? |

5

Conjoint Behavioral Consultation Research

CHAPTER OBJECTIVES

Upon completing this chapter, readers should be able to:

1. Describe findings from outcome-based conjoint behavioral consultation (CBC) research.
2. Explain important process variables to research in CBC, and describe findings from preliminary investigations.
3. Discuss the results of initial acceptability research in CBC.
4. Articulate important research directions in CBC.

INTRODUCTION

Several previous reviews of the consultation outcome research literature that have been published will not be discussed here (see Mannino & Shore, 1975; Medway, 1979, 1982; Medway & Updyke, 1985; Sibley, 1986). In addition, various methodological and conceptual issues in research on consultation have been discussed in detail (see Bergan & Kratochwill, 1990; Kratochwill et al., 1988). The research on teacher and parent training is also relevant to the consultation outcome literature, but is not discussed here. Recently, empirical studies in the area of CBC have been conducted to evaluate the effectiveness of the model for various target problems. Some preliminary research has also been conducted assessing the communication processes that have been identified in successful conjoint consultation cases. Likewise, one study evaluated a national sample of school psychologists' reported acceptability of the model. These studies are reviewed in this chapter.

OUTCOME RESEARCH

Outcome research assessing the effectiveness of CBC is accumulating. In an early study, Sheridan, Kratochwill, and Elliott (1990) were concerned with increasing the social initiation behaviors of socially withdrawn children. Of particular interest was the demonstration of behavioral generalization to the home setting. The participants in this study included four socially withdrawn children from a rural town in the midwest (3 girls, 1 boy; ages 8–12). Selection criteria included teacher referral, low scores on the Social Initiation subscale of a prepublication version of the Social Skills Rating System (SSRS) (Gresham & Elliott, 1990), direct observational data indicating low levels of social initiations toward peers, and parent and teacher interview data. There were two treatment conditions in the study (CBC and consultation with teachers only). In both conditions, a systematic behavioral consultation procedure (Kratochwill & Bergan, 1990) was followed. In the CBC condition, teachers and parents worked together with a school psychologist consultant; in the teacher-only condition, parents were not included in consultation. In both experimental conditions, children were exposed to the same behavioral treatment (goal setting, self-monitoring, and positive reinforcement). In the CBC condition, these same procedures were implemented across home and school settings. In teacher-only consultation, they were instituted at school only.

Sheridan et al. (1990) used multiple-baseline-across-participants designs to evaluate the effectiveness of the separate consultation interventions. Results of the study are presented in Figures 5.1 and 5.2. When consultation was undertaken with parents and teachers together, initiations increased in both home and school settings. Baseline performance for each child was approximately 1 initiation per week at school; during the last phase of treatment, performances increased to between 30 and 40 initiations per week. At home, baseline levels ranged from approximately 1 initiation per week to approximately 7 per week during the last phase of treatment.

However, when consultation was undertaken with teachers only, childrens' initiations increased at school only. Baseline performance for each child was 0 to 1 initiation per week at school, with weekly rates of between 6 and 26 during the last phase of treatment. At home, baseline rates were between 0 and 1.5 per week, increasing to between only 1 and 4 per week during the last phase of treatment. Treatment gains at school were maintained for all children in both conditions, but were most notable for those in the CBC condition.

In summary, this study was the first to investigate the efficacy of CBC using a standardized format following the Kratochwill and Bergan (1990) framework. In general, the traditional use of behavioral consultation with

Subject 1

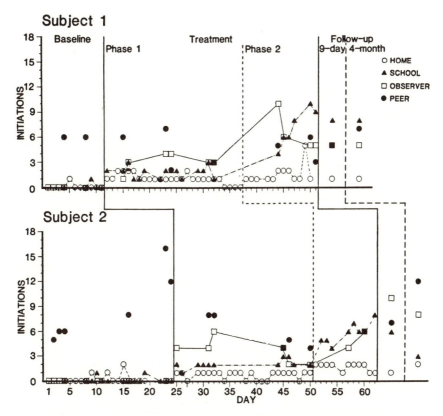

Figure 5.1. Social initiations made at home and school by Subjects 1 and 2 in CBC condition. (*Source*: Sheridan, S. M., Kratochwill, T. R., & Elliott, S. N. [1990]. Behavioral consultation with parents and teachers: Delivering treatment for socially withdrawn children at home and school. *School Psychology Review*, *19*, 33–52. Reproduced with permission.)

teachers was found to be effective in increasing the social initiation behaviors of socially withdrawn children at school. However, generalization of treatment effects to the home setting was demonstrated only when parents were actively involved in consultation and treatment. Maintenance of treatment effects also appeared to be stronger when conjoint consultation procedures were utilized. Social validity and treatment integrity measures were also included and yielded positive results.

Although the outcomes were positive with the conjoint approach, the results of the study do not negate the possibility that other generalization

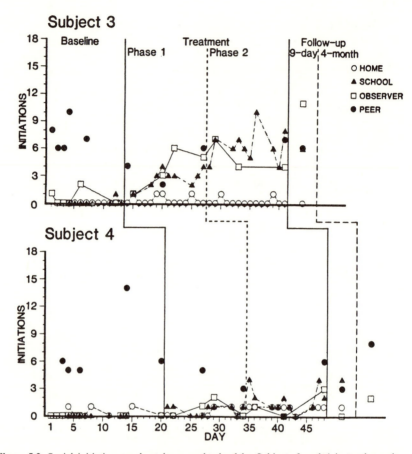

Figure 5.2. Social initiations made at home and school by Subjects 3 and 4 in teacher-only consultation condition. (*Source*: Sheridan, S. M., Kratochwill, T. R., & Elliott, S. N. [1990]. Behavioral consultation with parents and teachers: Delivering treatment for socially withdrawn children at home and school. *School Psychology Review, 19*, 33–52. Reproduced with permission.)

tactics would be equally or more effective than using another treatment agent. Moreover, some limitations were apparent, including the small number of subjects in each condition and limited follow-up data.

A second outcome study evaluated the effects of CBC combined with a behavioral training and reinforcement program with three Caucasian boys between the ages of 8 and 9 diagnosed with attention deficit–hyperactivity disorder (ADHD) and exhibiting performance deficits in their cooperative play behavior (Colton, Sheridan, Jenson, & Malm, 1995). Parents were three Caucasian mothers of the students who were living in low socioeconomic conditions. Teachers were three Caucasians teaching 2nd and 3rd grade at two different elementary schools located in a large urban area. A behavioral social skills treatment package was implemented within the context of CBC to address the children's observed social deficits.

The CBC procedures used the Kratochwill and Bergan format as extended by Sheridan et al. (1990). The behavioral social skills treatment program consisted of four major components: (1) social skills coaching and role play, (2) a home–school communication system, (3) self-monitoring of recess behaviors, and (4) positive reinforcement. In general, each parent and teacher dyad jointly selected 7 social skills within the rubric of "cooperative play." These skills served as direct targets of training. The steps for each skill (adapted from McGinnis & Goldstein, 1984) were written on "Friendship Recipe Cards," which served as a medium for coaching. Coaching instructions were included with each Friendship Recipe Card to instruct parents and teachers in the appropriate procedures and to increase treatment integrity. For Participants 1 and 3, teachers provided coaching of each target skill. The teacher of Participant 2, however, indicated that she did not have adequate time to provide the coaching, so the procedure was carried out by his mother.

After the participant was coached in the skill identified on the Friendship Recipe Card (e.g., playing a game, problem solving, responding to teasing), he was responsible for practicing the skill. Specifically, each child was responsible for (1) self-monitoring his performance on the playground, (2) discussing it with his teacher and completing a home note, and (3) receiving positive reinforcement at home for achieving a predetermined number of points, practicing the "friendship skill recipes," discussing his performance with his parents, and returning the home note to school.

Outcome measures in this study included direct observations of positive interaction behaviors in analogue, and behavioral rating scales. Specifically, 20-minute *direct (partial interval) observations* were conducted one to two times weekly in analogue play situations to assess participants' positive interaction behaviors toward classmates. The analogue/naturalistic sessions were videotaped and observed by two blind, independent trained observers in random order, who also coded 33% of the same tapes for purposes of interrater reliability (overall, 92% agreement was achieved). Several *checklists and rating scales* including the SSRS—Teacher, Parent, and Student forms (Gresham & Elliott, 1990), the Child Behavior Checklist, Teacher Report Form, and Attention Deficit Disorders Scale were used for purposes of defining the participant pool.

Two forms of *social validity* were assessed in this study: social comparison and subjective evaluation (Kazdin, 1977). First, one same-gender classmate per subject, identified by classroom teachers as having adequate social skills (i.e., few or no problems interacting with peers) and involved in the analogue observations, served as comparisons. Data collected for these comparisons serve as a reference to determine the degree to which target participants' positive interactive behaviors corresponded to those of peers.

 Acceptability of CBC was assessed on the Behavior Intervention Rating System (revised for consultation procedures), completed by parents and teachers (Von Brock & Elliott, 1987). Child-subjects' acceptability of the treatment protocol was assessed by the Children's Intervention Rating Profile (CIRP) (Witt & Elliott, 1985). *Treatment integrity* was assessed for CBC procedures by systematic audiotape analysis. Integrity of parents' and teachers' follow-through of treatment procedures was assessed via self-report on the home note.

A *multiple-baseline-across-participants design* was used to evaluate the effects of the CBC/social skills treatment program on target childrens' cooperative play behaviors. Direct observational data for all three children are presented in Figure 5.3. All subjects increased positive play behaviors with peers during treatment phases. Data trends for Subjects 1 and 3 are generally in the positive direction, with a generally acceptable degree of variability within phases. There was no overlap between baseline and treatment data for Child 1, and the amount of overlap between baseline and treatment data for Child 3 is minimal. Taken together, behavioral data suggest that the CBC/social skills program exerted functional control for Children 1 and 3. On the other hand, Child 2's data were variable with a high degree of overlap, suggesting little experimental control. Further, all parent and teacher ratings on the SSRS (with the exception of the parent rating for Child 1) indicated positive increases in overall social skills scores from pre- to posttreatment.

Social comparison data suggested that all children demonstrated substantial behavioral gains and increased their positive interactions such that they approached the level of "normal" comparison peers. Regarding treatment acceptability, parents and teachers reported that the procedures were acceptable, and child responses suggested that they found the social skills intervention highly acceptable. Treatment integrity data indicated that the consultant achieved 98% of consultation objectives across all interviews and that parents and teachers adhered to treatment components 100% of the time.

In summary, Colton and colleagues furthered CBC research by demonstrating its utility for a limited number of students with ADHD experiencing difficulties with social interactions. Thus, it tested the model with a new

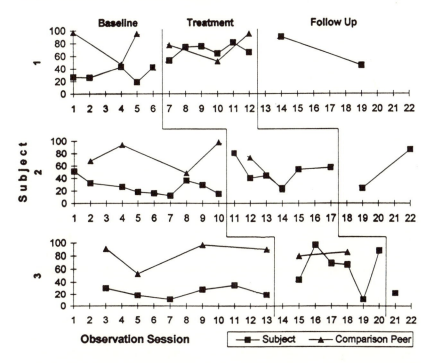

Figure 5.3. Percentage of cooperative play behaviors demonstrated by subjects receiving conjoint behavioral consultation services. (*Source*: Colton, D., Sheridan, S. M., Jenson, W. R., & Malm, K. [1995, March]. Behavioral consultation with parents and teachers: Promoting cooperative peer interactions with boys with ADHD. Paper presented at the annual meeting of the National Association of School Psychologists, Chicago, IL. Reproduced with permission.)

behavioral target and diagnostic group and involved parents from low socio-economic status conditions as consultees (although this was not a central or planned aspect of this study).

──────────────────── CASE STUDIES

Some CBC case studies have also been conducted. In an extensive, carefully controlled set of case studies, the model was evaluated with academically underachieving children (Galloway & Sheridan, 1994). Participants were six primary-grade students (grades 1–3) who often failed to complete math assignments on time and/or with acceptable levels of accuracy.

They all demonstrated performance deficits; they had the skills to complete assignments with accuracy, but often failed to do so. Likewise, the children demonstrated variable performance that was resistant to previous documented intervention attempts.

In two separate sets of case studies, the investigators evaluated the effectiveness of a standard intervention with and without the inclusion of CBC. Both studies involved the use of a home note, wherein teachers recorded subjects' daily performances in math, as well as process behaviors intended to help them complete work (e.g., pencil ready, papers out). The home note also included a checklist to help remind parents of what to do at home and served as a measure of treatment integrity.

A manual was developed that instructed parents in the use of the home note, including potential reinforcers and ways to handle problems. In the first set of case studies, the manual and home note served as the only interventions. In the second set, the home note and manual were used, but were instituted in the context of CBC. Students were also involved in the latter part of consultation (plan implementation and treatment evaluation).

The investigators used AB with replication designs to assess outcomes of the home note and CBC interventions. Data from these sets of case studies are presented in Figures 5.4 and 5.5. All three children in the home-note-only case studies showed improvements in math completion and accuracy. Baseline accuracy scores ranged from 43% to 69%, with posttreatment scores ranging from 67% to 83% (between 20% and 84% gains over baseline). Consistent with the selection criteria, baseline data paths were unstable (i.e., fewer than 80% of the data points were within 15% of the mean level). Furthermore, the data remained variable during treatment. Baseline completion levels were variable and ranged from 43% to 74%, with posttreatment completion rates ranging from 86% to 88%. Completion data for two of the three children in the first set of case studies continued to be variable after treatment.

As in the home-note condition, all children in the home-note-with-CBC condition demonstrated improvements in math completion and accuracy, but the gains were greater and more stable. Specifically, baseline accuracy means ranged from 35% to 57%, with treatment means ranging from 86% to 89%

Figure 5.4. Completion and accuracy rates for subjects receiving home-note intervention. (*Source*: Galloway, J., & Sheridan, S. M. [1994]. Implementing scientific practices through case studies: Examples using home–school interventions and consultation. *Journal of School Psychology, 32,* 385–413. Reproduced with permission.)

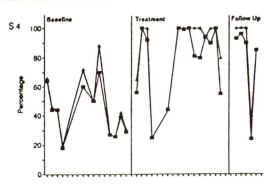

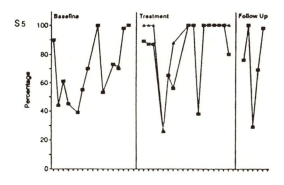

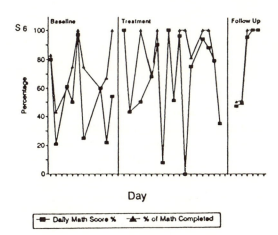

Day

◼ Daily Math Score %   ▲ % of Math Completed

(representing up to a 149% gain over baseline). Although baseline performance was variable, the improved performance during treatment was considered stable for all three children. Regarding work completion, baseline means ranged from 41% to 69%, with treatment means ranging from 95% to 100%. As with the accuracy data, completion data were considered stable. Findings in the CBC case studies also suggested enhanced treatment integrity, maintenance of treatment gains at follow-up, and consumer acceptability. Furthermore, parents in the CBC condition adhered more faithfully to the treatment regimen than did parents in the home-note-only case studies, which may be one reason for the greater treatment effects. Parents in the CBC case studies also used home reinforcers more effectively than did parents in the home-note-only condition. Teachers in the CBC condition reported greater satisfaction; however, there was no difference in the degree of treatment integrity demonstrated by teachers.

In sum, for students with a history of social and academic performance problems who had not responded to traditional intervention strategies, the addition of consultation with parents and teachers appeared to have enhanced treatment outcomes. Maintenance and generalization of treatment gains appeared to be stronger when more intensive consultation procedures were utilized (i.e., when parents were actively involved in consultation and treatment). On the basis of the findings of Galloway and Sheridan (1994), this result does not appear to be due simply to the provision of information. It is possible that the improvement factors may be related to the relationship that develops among participants in the CBC process; however, this is an empirical question in need of research.

Another case study involved a child with irrational fears (Sheridan & Colton, 1994). Specifically, a kindergarten teacher referred a 6-year-old boy who spoke of nightmares repeatedly in school. The boy reported vivid stories of monsters and spiders in his room that often grabbed him by the ankle. He was terrified of sleeping alone and as a result slept in his parents' room all night, every night, for more than 2 years. The goal for consultation in this case was to get the child to sleep in his own room on a consistent basis.

Treatment involved a fading of environment and positive reinforcement procedure, wherein positive reinforcers were delivered each time the child slept in a spot that moved successively closer to his own room. Direct

Figure 5.5. Completion and accuracy rates for subjects receiving conjoint behavioral consultation with home–note intervention. (*Source*: Galloway, J., & Sheridan, S. M. [1994]. Implementing scientific practices through case studies: Examples using home-school interventions and consultation. *Journal of School Psychology, 32*, 385–413. Reproduced with permission.)

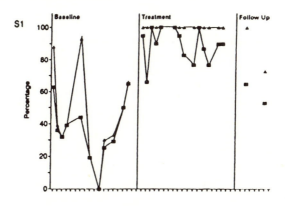

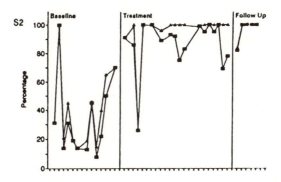

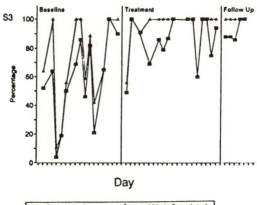

Day

-■- Daily Math Score %   -▲- % of Math Completed

observational data, collected by the boy's mother, are presented in Figure 5.6. An AB case study design was used, with the criterion being adequate performance demonstrated over two occasions at each successive level.

Dramatic, immediate improvements were seen in this case. Two weeks of baseline showed 0 occasions of sleeping in his own room and 14 occasions of sleeping on the floor of his parents' room. Seven steps were identified during treatment, which involved the child moving successively closer to and finally into his own room. As can be seen in Figure 5.6, the child demonstrated immediate effects, with perfect performance at each level. Likewise, he demonstrated no regression at a 1-month follow-up.

This case study demonstrated significant and immediate effects with a very different type of behavioral problem not typically dealt with in school settings. Unfortunately, because the consultation occurred at the end of the school year, there are no follow-up data on the child's irrational fears at school.

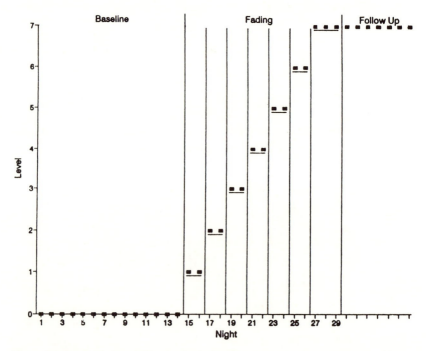

Figure 5.6. Data depicting Mark's sleeping in locations that successively approximate his own bedroom. (*Source*: Sheridan, S. M., & Colton, D. L. [1994]. Conjoint behavioral consultation: A review and case study. *Journal of Educational and Psychological Consultation, 5*, 211–228. Reproduced with permission.)

Some research has been conducted assessing verbal processes in CBC. Sheridan (1994) reported a study that investigated consultant and consultee statements in CBC compared to statements made in consultation with teachers only. The verbal behaviors were analyzed in relation to some of the unique goals of CBC (i.e., increased communication with and about family and child; shared responsibility for problem identification across home and school settings; active parental involvement in problem-solving process). Specifically, it was hypothesized that (1) there would be more statements about background environment and behavior setting in CBC than in traditional teacher-only consultation; (2) parent consultees would emit an approximately equal number of utterances as teacher consultees; (3) the proportion of statements from teachers would be significantly less in CBC interviews than in teacher-only consultation interviews; and (4) a greater proportion of consultant elicitors would be present in CBC interviews than in teacher-only interviews.

Verbatim transcripts of Conjoint Problem Identification Interviews from six cases were analyzed. The interviews were coded using the Consultation Analysis Record (Bergan & Tombari, 1976), which allows for the categorization of each thought unit in terms of its source, content, process, and control characteristics. Means of statements made within each category by each participant were compared to those reported in previous research that analyzed verbal processes in teacher-only consultation (i.e., Martens, Lewandowski, & Houk, 1989).

Results of the descriptive analysis both supported and contradicted the research hypotheses. Contrary to predictions, there was no difference found in the amount of statements made regarding background environment and behavior setting in the CBC transcripts as compared to teacher-only consultation transcripts. The proportions of background environment verbalizations in CBC were 0.05, 0.07 and 0.08 in CBC for consultants, teachers, and parents, respectively, and less than 0.035 and 0.05 for consultants and teachers in teacher-only consultation. The proportions of behavior setting statements were 0.25, 0.26, and 0.28 for consultants, teachers, and parents in CBC, respectively, and 0.32 and 0.35 for consultants and teachers in teacher-only consultation interviews.

Figure 5.7 depicts the percentages of total statements made by each participant in CBC. Consistent with research predictions was the finding that parents were actively involved in problem-identification interviews. In fact, parents contributed a percentage of verbalizations slightly greater than that

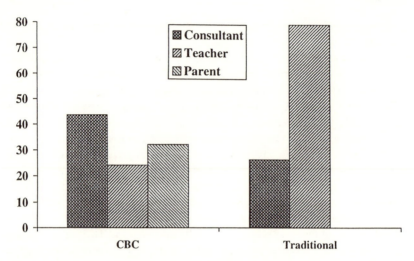

Figure 5.7. Percentage of total statements made by each participant in CBC compared to traditional teacher-only consultation. (*Source*: Sheridan, S. M. [1994, August]. Conceptual and empirical bases of conjoint behavioral consultation. Invited address presented at the annual meeting of the American Psychological Association, Los Angeles, CA. Reproduced with permission.)

contributed by teachers in CBC interviews (0.32 and 0.24 of the total statements were provided by parents and teachers, respectively). Their involvement was directly elicited (i.e., 50% of elicitors were directed toward the parent), and they appeared to provide a substantial portion of information. This finding supports the CBC objective of obtaining information from parents and promoting their active involvement in problem solving.

Also consistent with predictions, the teacher's role appeared to be different in CBC than in teacher-only consultation. Specifically, the teacher's verbal contribution to discussions in CBC was proportionately less than in consultation wherein the teacher served as the sole consultee (0.24 of all statements in CBC were made by teachers, vs. 0.74 in teacher-only consultation). Interestingly, teachers were found to ask proportionately more questions in CBC than in teacher-only consultation (7% elicitors in CBC vs. 1% in teacher-only consultation), and consultants used proportionately fewer elicitors in CBC (19%) than in teacher-only consultation (34%). This finding suggests that teachers may perceive their role in CBC as one of shared responsibility for eliciting information from parents in CBC. However, it should be recognized that these data are purely descriptive and do not imply statistically significant differences.

Finally, an unexpected finding regarding the consultant's role in CBC emerged from the process analysis. Specifically, consultants tended to control more of the discussion in CBC. Specifically, 56% of the statements made in CBC interviews were made by consultants, as compared to 26% in teacher-only consultation. Of all elicitors in the interviews, 79% were made by the consultant (similar data are unavailable for teacher-only consultation interviews). It may be that the added complexity of a second consultee (i.e., parent) encouraged consultants to make deliberate and active attempts to structure the discussion.

ACCEPTABILITY RESEARCH

An important issue pertaining to the application of CBC is its acceptability in practice. A national survey of nationally certified school psychologists investigating the acceptability of CBC by school psychologists was completed by Sheridan and Steck (1995). Using items from the Behavioral Intervention Rating Scale, the acceptability of CBC in relation to consultant variables (age, level of training, years of experience, theoretical orientation, age of student served) and perceived logistical barriers (time, administrative support) was investigated. Also assessed was the differential acceptability of CBC in contrast to other modes of service delivery (direct service and teacher- and parent-only consultation) for academic, behavioral, and social–emotional problems.

The results of the survey were very supportive of CBC as a consultation service-delivery model. School psychologists rated CBC as very acceptable (mean = 4.2 on a 5-point Likert scale of acceptability). Their ratings of the acceptability of CBC were most affected by external constraints of time concerns and perceived administrative/organizational support for implementing the procedure. Age of students served, theoretical orientation, years of experience, and level of training had little if any impact on the acceptability ratings.

It was found that CBC was rated as more acceptable than any other mode of service delivery across problem types (see Figure 5.8). Further, CBC was rated essentially the same across all problem types, suggesting that CBC was perceived as more generally applicable than had been anticipated. Another important finding was that the age of student served did not appear to influence acceptability ratings of mode of service delivery, with the exception that school psychologists who serve secondary students rated direct service and CBC approximately equally (see Figure 5.9).

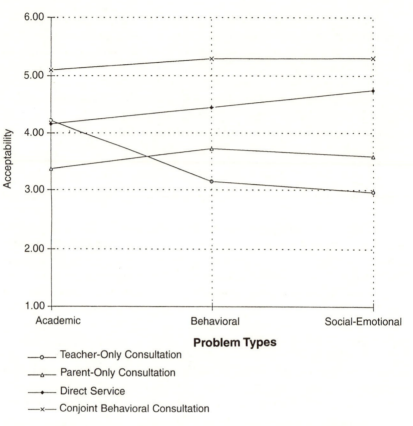

Figure 5.8. Mean acceptability ratings of CBC, teacher-only consultation, parent-only consult-ation, and direct service. (*Source*: Sheridan, S. M., & Steck, M. [1995]. Acceptability of conjoint behavioral consultation: A national survey of school psychologists. *School Psychology Review*. Reproduced with permission.)

RESEARCH DIRECTIONS

Research in conjoint behavioral consultation is accumulating, with generally positive and encouraging results. There are several areas in need of investigation to further its empirical base. First, it seems necessary at this time to systematically investigate the utility of the model with children presenting various personal characteristics. For example, the usefulness of CBC with children from various ethnic, educational, and socioeconomic backgrounds has not been evaluated. Colton and colleagues' sample was comprised of families in low socioeconomic conditions; however, this was not a central aspect of the study and was not controlled carefully. Given the emphasis on including all parents in the educational process (including those from different cultural and ethnic groups), it is necessary to determine those practices that are more or less effective with diverse families.

A second research direction should focus on systematically assessing relationship variables in CBC. For example, research that evaluates the short-term and long-term effects of conjoint problem solving on the home–school relationship could be conducted. Specific research on the generalization of the parent–teacher relationship over time is a particular interest in light of the goals of CBC. Likewise, most participants in previous research have demonstrated a willingness to engage in the process. Process and outcome researchers should begin to investigate consultation sessions under conditions where consultees have a history of interpersonal problems, lack the motivation to work together, or exhibit resistance to the collaborative process.

An additional research direction concerns alternative parent, teacher, and child roles in conjoint consultation. Previous process research suggested that the teacher's role in CBC may be qualitatively different than in other forms of teacher-only consultation. It is possible that teachers could be trained to serve as consultants with parents and allow consultant-specialists to transition more quickly out of certain consultation sessions. Likewise, it is possible that not all parents and teachers will be able to adopt a high level of participation (i.e., ongoing consultation interviews and meetings). Procedures that allow consultants to determine the essential points at which all participants must be involved and points at which progress can be made with only a teacher or parent present would be necessary. Finally, some research (e.g., Galloway & Sheridan, 1994) included children in the final phase of the Conjoint Problem Analysis Interview (CPAI) and Conjoint Treatment Evaluation Interview (CTEI) to involve them in plan specification, to help them understand intervention procedures, and to assess their perceptions of outcomes. Alternative roles for clients, including their active involvement in various aspects of the consultation sessions, may be an interesting line of inquiry.

As currently practiced, conjoint consultation services are typically offered to address presenting problems when no alternative intervention programs are in place. It may be desirable to initiate the model in cases where an alternative treatment program is in place. In these cases, the primary goal of CBC may be generalization of effects to other, nontreatment settings. For example, social skills training is typically provided in small groups to four or

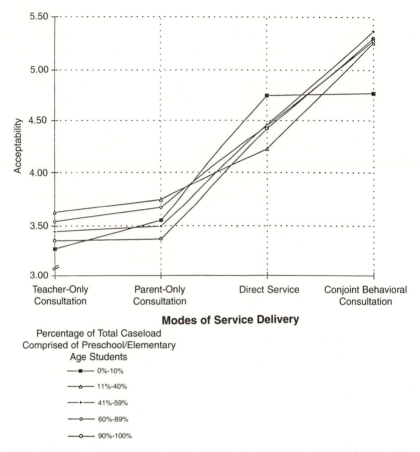

Modes of Service Delivery

Percentage of Total Caseload
Comprised of Preschool/Elementary
Age Students

——■—— 0%-10%

——△—— 11%-40%

——•—— 41%-59%

——◇—— 60%-89%

——○—— 90%-100%

Figure 5.9. Mean acceptability ratings of modes of service delivery for school psychologists who serve in preschool, elementary, middle, and secondary school settings.

more students. A major limitation of many social skills programs is their inability to demonstrate generalization of learned social skills to the natural environment (DuPaul & Eckert, 1994). CBC may be particularly relevant in encouraging extension of students' use of social skills to the classroom and home settings.

A final research direction concerns furthering the investigation of CBC processes and acceptability. For example, the preliminary study of CBC verbal processes was conducted with only six CPIIs of successful cases. It would be necessary to replicate the study using a larger sample. Likewise, it is necessary to evaluate transcripts of cases where consultation goals were not met, outcomes were limited, or consultee resistance was a factor. Acceptability research must also be extended to alternative roles and participants beyond school psychologists. For example, it is important to obtain a large-scale sample of teachers and parents who may serve as consultees and solicit their perceptions of the model.

DISCUSSION QUESTIONS

1	What types of research designs have typically been used in conjoint behavioral consultation outcome research? What are the major findings?
2	What are some ways in which verbal behaviors of consultants and consultees differ between CBC and consultation with teachers only?
3	What additional process research might be conducted?
4	What are some identified variables that contribute (and variables that do not contribute) to school psychologists' acceptance of CBC?
5	What are some important research directions in CBC?

6

Conjoint Behavioral Consultation Case Studies

CHAPTER OBJECTIVES

Upon completing this chapter the reader should be able to:

1. Describe various applications of conjoint behavioral consultation (CBC) as they relate to different client characteristics and target behaviors.
2. Identify several relevant examples from cases that highlight important benefits of CBC.
3. Discuss procedures by which various measures can be combined to assess CBC outcomes.

INTRODUCTION TO CHAPTER

In this chapter, we present several case scenarios illustrating the procedures of CBC. The cases represent scientist-practitioner models of service delivery, incorporating careful and systematic assessment procedures that are linked directly to intervention and evaluation.

Several specific and important aspects of the cases should be highlighted. First, the cases represent the manner in which behavioral interview procedures can be combined with a range of other behavioral assessment methods, collected across sources and settings to obtain comprehensive data. Second, the cases illustrate the utility of assessment and the procedures by which data lead directly to treatment plans. Third, systematic case study evaluation procedures were used to determine plan effectiveness in a quasi-experimental manner. Furthermore, these evaluation procedures were carried out within the naturalistic settings of the home and school. Finally, the cases incorporated various methods to increase ecological validity of the results, including assessment of maintenance, treatment acceptability, treatment integrity, and social validity (Gresham, 1991).

SOCIAL WITHDRAWAL: THE CASE OF SHERRY

Background Information

Sherry is a 9-year-old, 3rd-grade student with average intellectual and language abilities. She and her twin brother are the oldest of four children. Although Sherry appeared to be well liked, she interacted little with peers. Furthermore, her interactions were generally in response to initiations made by others. Both at home and at school, she initiated very few interactions (e.g., conversations or activities) with peers.

Given Sherry's difficulties across settings, a CBC approach was adopted. The stages of consultation included problem identification, problem analysis, treatment implementation, treatment evaluation, and follow-up. Through a conjoint approach, Sherry's social difficulties were addressed in a joint, cooperative problem-solving effort on the part of a consultant, Sherry's parents, and her teacher.

Problem Identification

Several methods were used to define and assess the specific target behavior to be addressed in consultation, including conjoint interviews with Sherry's teacher and mother, direct observations of Sherry's social initiation behaviors across settings, behavioral rating scales (Social Skills Rating Scale-Parent and Teacher Forms, [SSRS-P, SSRS-T]) (Gresham & Elliott, 1990), a sociometric technique (Barclay Classroom Assessment Scale) (Barclay, 1978), and a self-report rating scale (Self-Perception Profile for Children [SPPC]) (Harter, 1985).

A Conjoint Problem Identification Interview (CPII) was conducted with Sherry's mother and teacher to discuss concerns regarding Sherry's social behaviors at home and at school. During the CPII, both consultees expressed their primary concern as being Sherry's low level of initiating interactions with peers. Both home and in school, Sherry typically waited for others to approach her or to initiate an activity. Although Sherry generally responded positively, she reportedly rarely or never spontaneously started a conversation or activity with others. As a result, Sherry often sat or walked alone during play times, unless peers approached her and suggested an activity.

During the CPII, Sherry's mother reported that Sherry's twin brother often initiated activities or responded for Sherry when approached by others at home. Her mother stated that her brother's dominance may have contributed to the development of a nonassertive behavioral style in Sherry. Sherry's teacher reported ssimilar behavior pattern; however, it was not considered a "problem" at school until knowledge of the pervasiveness of this behavior was shared by Sherry's mother. In fact, Sherry's brother was accepted as the "leader" of the two at school, and this acceptance may have been inadvertently reinforced. The behaviors of Sherry's brother (established early at home) may have been a setting event for her lack of social initiations across settings.

Direct observations were conducted by Sherry's mother and teacher daily to monitor her social initiation behaviors at home and school. Likewise, 30-minute direct observations were conducted twice weekly by an independent observer at school throughout all stages of consultation. These repeated observations were conducted to obtain direct measures of Sherry's social initiations and related behavior patterns over time and settings.

On all of the behavioral checklists and rating scales, Sherry's social initiative behaviors were reported to be deficient. Patterns of subscale responses on the SSRS-P and SSRS-T indicated difficulties initiating peer interactions, relative to other social skill areas. Specific items that were rated by both Sherry's parents and teacher as never or only sometimes true included "Initiates conversations with others rather than waiting for others to talk first" and "Introduces herself to new people without being told to do so." Similarly, Sherry was nominated most often by her classmates on a sociometric nomination technique (Barclay, 1978) on a subset of items assessing shy and withdrawn behaviors. She was rated as the "most quiet in class" by 76% of her classmates, and She also rated herself on that item. On the SPPC, Sherry acknowledged not having many friends, desiring to have more friends, and usually doing things by herself.

The general behavior that was chosen for intervention was Sherry's low level of initiating interactions with peers. This behavior was defined operationally as "approaching a peer and emitting a question or making a statement, clearly suggesting mutual participation in an activity, or requesting a response from the peer." Goals established by Sherry's mother and teacher during the CPII were 3 initiations at school and 1 initiation at home per day. An excerpt from the CPII involving Sherry's mother, teacher, and school psychologist is presented below.

Consultant: So it sounds like both of you are really concerned about Sherry being able to take the first step...about initiating interactions or conversations with her peers, rather than waiting to be approached by someone else.
Teacher: Mm hmm.
Parent: Right.

Later in interview:

Consultant: In terms of where you're seeing the problems, you're seeing them here at school, and you're seeing it at home. Where at school do you see the greatest difficulty initiating interactions?
Teacher: Well, during our independent time she...today for the first time in her whole third- grade life she chose somebody to start a contract game with. It never happened before.
Consultant: Typically she wouldn't do that?
Teacher: No, she'd never, ever done it before, and there have been other contracts. And if someone came to get her she got that twosome part of her contract done, but if no one came to get her, I think she just waited. Beth always made sure.... Sooner or later Beth always starts.
Consultant: Where else?
Teacher: Well, down at lunch. That's such a nonthreatening situation that I would expect if I was going to see her initiate something, any time, that would be when. And she'll join a conversation good but she's not a conversation starter.
Consultant: How about at home? Or in nonschool situations — where do you see the problems?
Parent: Well, she doesn't like to go to other kids' houses. I think it's the idea of the parents, you know, the fact that there's going to be strange adults there. Probably that's what makes her nervous.
Teacher: I think you're right. I really think you're right.
Consultant: So, less familiar adults.
Parent: Yeah. She'll be pleasant, she'll smile, but she won't say much. They really have to ask her a direct question. She won't start up anything and she won't volunteer information usually. They've got to, not quite pry it out of her, but...
Consultant: Is that true within your house as well? When they come over to visit you?
Parent: Yeah. If they come to our house, she's still pretty quiet. It's better, but she usually waits for them to start the conversation.

And waits for them to ask her a direct question before she'll volunteer information. If she gets a chance. See a lot of the time, her brother doesn't give her a chance. I think she kind of waits and lets Philip do the talking. Part of this may be being a twin and letting him do the talking for her. It's gotten to be a habit.

Consultant: That's really interesting. Now, we want to start working on Sherry's beginning conversations. Do you think it would be most easy to begin working right within your own home when people come over, or when she wants people to come over to visit for her to...

Parent: Have her do the inviting. Yeah.

Consultant: And at school, we talked about the lunchroom, the classroom, playground.... Where would you like to prioritize...to begin?

Teacher: I think the place to start would be in the cooperative learning circles because those are already established, and I think it would be a very nonthreatening environment for her to improve on her social skills.

A number of interesting and important observations can be made in relation to this brief excerpt. Early on, the consultant takes time to establish agreement between the consultees on the specific problem issues to be addressed through consultation. She also illustrates how information can be obtained across home and school settings.

As the interview progresses, the importance of including both Sherry's parent and her teacher in the consultation process is highlighted. For example, her mother's observation that "strange adults...[make] her nervous" is confirmed by her teacher, who may not have been aware of this behavioral manifestation. Likewise, the notion that Sherry may wait and allow her twin brother to speak for her represents an important issue that is identified by Sherry's mother. This potentially critical information would not have been available without active parental involvement in the problem-identification stage.

Problem Analysis and Treatment Implementation

A Conjoint Problem Analysis Interview (CPAI) was conducted to review baseline data and confirm or disconfirm the existence of a problem across settings. During 2 weeks of direct observations, independent probes of Sherry's social behaviors at school revealed zero initiations made toward peers. Baseline observations conducted daily by Sherry's mother and teacher suggested 1 initiation at home and 1 at school, during 1 week of data collection. Thus, development and implementation of a treatment plan to be instituted across settings was warranted.

A treatment package was developed and implemented in two phases to increase Sherry's social initiation behaviors. Identical procedures were instituted at home and at school, and Sherry's mother and teacher were provided with treatment manuals to maximize treatment consistency and integrity.

The treatment package was implemented in two general phases. Phase 1 consisted of three primary components: goal-setting, self-report, and positive reinforcement procedures. Phase 2 involved self-monitoring and positive reinforcement.

In the *goal-setting procedures*, Sherry was actively involved in setting goals to initiate interactions with peers. Specifically, a "goal sheet" was developed, on which Sherry and her teacher established daily goals at school, and Sherry and her mother established daily goals at home. Examples of goals included "ask(ing) Jenny to play jumprope at recess," and "call(ing) Stephanie on the phone to ask about a record." Sherry set the majority of goals herself, without the need for prompting by her teacher or parents.

Self-reporting occurred in conjunction with goal-setting to encourage Sherry to monitor her own social behaviors. Specifically, Sherry recorded attainment of her goals in a separate column on her goal sheets. She also recorded the time and participants involved to monitor qualitative aspects of the interactions. At the end of each day, Sherry showed the goal sheet to her teacher at school and mother at home, who provided praise and encouragement for continued goal attainment.

Positive reinforcement was provided by Sherry's mother and teacher at several levels, including verbal praise for all instances of social initiations and stickers and written comments on goal sheets. Backup reinforcers were also delivered for successful attainment of increasing numbers of goals. Attainment of each goal at home and at school earned 1 point, and Sherry received a concrete reinforcer upon attainment of a given number of points. Points earned at school and at home were combined, and delivery of all concrete reinforcers occurred at home.

Sherry's mother, teacher, and an independent observer continued to monitor all instances of initiations made by Sherry at home and at school. During this phase of treatment, Sherry's mother observed between 0 and 3 initiations daily, with an average of 1 per day. Daily initiations observed by Sherry's teacher at school ranged from 1 to 3, with an average of 1.8 per day. Because the daily goals were 3 initiations at school and 1 at home, the behavioral goals were only partially met. Therefore, modifications in the initial program were indicated.

The primary component of Phase 2 of the treatment program was *self-monitoring*. An overall goal of "starting conversations, games, or activities with several friends or classmates each day" was established, and Sherry self-monitored all initiations toward peers at home and at school in a special notebook. She shared the notebook with her teacher and her mother, who provided verbal praise for the number of initiations made across settings. Each initiation earned 1 point, and Sherry chose a reinforcer to work toward upon earning a given number of points. Again, all reinforcers were delivered at home.

Home-school communication was essential throughout all phases of consultation and treatment. This communication involved conjoint consultation meetings and a daily review of Sherry's progress across both settings by Sherry's mother and teacher. Thus, along with monitoring school behaviors, Sherry's teacher reviewed and praised her daily progress at home. Likewise, along with monitoring home behaviors, Sherry's mother reviewed and praised her daily progress at school. Sherry's mother and teacher also provided written comments on her goal sheets to maintain communication between themselves. An excerpt from the CPAI participated in by Sherry's mother, teacher, and school psychologist is presented below.

Consultant: ... Let's look at what we have here.

Parent: Not a lot.

Consultant: Monday it looks like she played with Helen, but Helen came over.

Parent: Helen did come over both times. She went home twice within about an hour. She thinks she might find something better to do if she goes home. And if she doesn't find anything better to do she'll come back. It's kind of hard on Sherry sometimes.

Consultant: Yeah, I bet.

Parent: Sherry knows that she really doesn't have to leave for the reason she gives. She even said one day, "Helen doesn't like me, she just comes over here because she's bored."

Consultant: What happened on these days? Tuesday and Thursday?

Parent: We just were home with nobody coming over. It was just her brother and sister.

Consultant: Okay.... You did a great job! That's exactly what we talked about. Would you say this was a typical week?

Parent: Pretty typical, yeah.

Consultant
(to teacher): Why don't we see what you have for last week?
  Teacher: Okay. I didn't really see any initiations Thursday, Friday, or Monday. But Tuesday we had a cooperative reading assignment, and Sherry's group was stumped and it took about three tries, but she was the only one who really came up with an answer. And when she finally realized that nobody else had an answer except her, then she did tell Jon an appropriate answer to the question. I really can't remember what the question was at that point. But it was a more structured cooperative reading assignment and her job was to help the group members out, which she did. Then Wednesday she asked Beth a question at lunch. And then later on in that same lunch period she told Chrissy a story.
  Consultant: What happened before she began an initiation?
  Teacher: For the first time, when she asked Beth a question, I didn't see anything. For the other one, we were all sharing stories about different things that happened at home with brothers and sisters. And then she thought up a story of her own and that was kind of a group discussion on troubles with brothers and sisters, basically.
  Parent: She probably has lots of those stories!
  Teacher: Each girl said some little thing they had happen and then Sherry took her turn, I mean it wasn't all that structured.
  Consultant: Was it prompted?
  Teacher: No, no. It was all on her own.
  Consultant: Great. So if she has something to contribute, or if she has an idea about it...
  Teacher: Mm hmm.
  Parent: I think especially if she's real sure about it. If she has any question that it's not the right thing then I don't think she'll say it. If she's hesitant at all that it may be wrong...she'll never want to give a wrong answer.
  Teacher: Yeah, exactly. Good point! I think it also depends on the group in which she's in. She doesn't feel the least bit threatened in the group with Jon, Justin, Heather, and herself. And I think that helps. When she works cooperatively with some of the girls outside of her social circle she's a lot more quiet.
  Consultant: Okay, so some of the things that facilitate her opening up and initiating something both at school and at home are things like being confident about what she's talking about and being com-

fortable with the people that she's with. Or being in a situation where it's a more accepted, structured, and appropriate thing to do. And those are some of the things that have been going on when you noticed her doing this.

Teacher: Yes.

Parent: Mm hmm.

Examination of this CPAI excerpt can help illustrate some important points regarding the conjoint consultation process. First, baseline data collected across settings are analyzed, with particular attention to conditions that may have facilitated Sherry's initiation of an interaction. Involving both the parent and teacher served an instrumental function in the interview. For example, Sherry's hesitance at providing wrong answers (antecedent condition) and the influence of her peer group (sequential condition) are important observations provided by both consultees. Thus, statements and observations of one consultee were validated and elaborated upon by the other, providing a broader and more accurate perspective on the problem. Likewise, direct communication between Sherry's mother and teacher was evident at important points in this interview, enhancing the dialogue and interpersonal relationship between these parties.

Treatment Evaluation

Multiple methods were used to determine the overall effectiveness of treatment, including direct observations, behavioral interviews, and behavioral rating scales. Direct observational data are provided in Figure 6.1. Information obtained through all measures indicated increases in Sherry's level of social initiations at both home and school.

A Conjoint Treatment Evaluation Interview (CTEI) was conducted 8 days after treatment modifications were instituted. At this meeting, both her mother and her teacher expressed great improvements in Sherry's overall social and emotional behaviors in conjunction with the treatment plan. A review of observational data collected by her mother at home revealed a range of 1-5 initiations, with an average of 2 per day. Initiations observed by her teacher at school revealed a range of 4-10, with an average of 7.17 per day. Likewise, independent observations at school revealed a range of 5-10 initiations toward peers, with an average of 6.5 per observation.

The SSRS-P, SSRS-T, and SPPC were readministered following treatment. Increases in ratings of Sherry's behaviors were noted at several levels

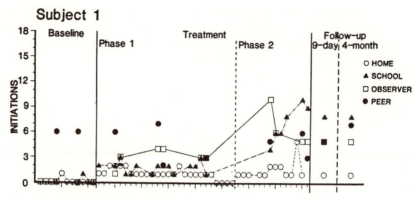

Figure 6.1. Frequency of social initiations made by Sherry and a comparison peer across home and school settings. (*Source:* Sheridan, S. M., Kratochwill, T. R., & Elliott, S. N. [1990]. Behavioral consultation with parents and teachers: Delivering treatment for socially withdrawn children at home and school. *School Psychology Review, 19,* 33–52. Reprinted with permission.)

following treatment. The greatest changes were noted on parent, teacher, and self-ratings of Sherry's social initiation behaviors.

Because the initial goals of initiating 1 interaction at home and 3 interactions at school per day were exceeded, procedures to fade program components were discussed. Specifically, concrete reinforcers were discontinued. Sherry continued to monitor her own initiations indefinitely (upon her own discretion), and home-school communication continued on an intermittent basis to monitor maintenance of treatment effects across settings. An excerpt from the CTEI involving Sherry's parent, teacher, and school psychologist follows.

Consultant: How did things go?
Parent: Pretty good. I think she's kind of excited about it.
Consultant: Good!
Parent: I don't have to remind her to do these things when she gets home. She's like, "Mom, it's four o'clock, I've got to..." or "Mom, I'm going to do this." She's real gung ho.
Consultant: Really?
Teacher: In school, too, though I see a very low-key enthusiasm. But I never have to remind her to set her goals for the day.
Consultant: Mm hmm.
Parent: She's excited. In fact, she set the goals for the whole week right away. And she made them all. And she's got tomorrow's set

already. Today, she already talked to Helen, so this has been met. And she made the comment, "Maybe this means in fourth grade I won't be so shy."

Consultant: Oh boy!

Teacher: Oh!

Parent: And she knows we're all trying to help, and I think she wants it to work. That's a big part of it.

Later in interview:

Consultant: When we first got together and talked about what it was we wanted to work towards, you both said to initiate one interaction a day would be good. It looks like Sherry is now doing that. Do you think we've met that goal pretty consistently?

Teacher: Yeah, I think so.

Parent: Basically it's worked out perfectly every time. There's been a couple...one time she made a call and had to talk to Beth's mom. And then Beth called her back because she was outside. Gee, that's good that she spoke to her mom, you know.

Consultant: Yes!... Do you think it is this program that has been helpful in getting Sherry to initiate these interactions?

Parent: Yeah, I think it probably is. Having it in black and white, so to speak...

Teacher: And it gives her a reason to try. Just wanting it isn't really enough. And having all the rewards delivered at home is a big help.

Consultant: She must feel pretty good, too. Would you like to keep something like this in effect, or modify it somehow?

Parent: Yeah, it is almost too easy, but yet, I don't want to push her and spoil it.

Teacher: Well, at school I could see increasing it to twice a day, but I wouldn't want to increase it to three times a day because we don't always have an afternoon recess.

Consultant: So all her goals are during recess time?

Teacher: Yes, I think they've all been during recess.

Consultant: One way that we might modify it is to establish one overall goal for her, and that is to "start conversations or ask friends to play," with no set limit imposed. She can keep track of her initiations herself. We might still require a minimum of two per day at school and home to ensure progress, but she could actually make several initiations both on the playground, in the classroom, and at home. And each one could be worth a point or sticker that she's saving toward her bigger weekly reward.

Parent: So she could get her reward faster if she did more.

Teacher: I like that idea really well.

This brief excerpt illustrates important aspects of the CTEI, especially as conducted in conjoint consultation. First, the importance of including the parent in the process is made clear early on. Specifically, her observations of Sherry's behaviors allow the consultant and consultees to assess immediate responsiveness to treatment. This is important treatment information that would not be available had the parent not been present in consultation.

It can be recalled that shared responsibility in treatment implementation and problem resolution is one of the primary goals of parent-teacher consultation. This goal is highlighted in the teacher's comment that "having all the rewards delivered at home is a big help." Finally, delineation of program modifications is made clear toward the end of this excerpt, giving the parent and teacher an opportunity to respond to structured means of strengthening the intervention.

Follow-up

Two follow-up evaluations were conducted following termination of treatment (at 9 days and 4 months). These evaluations consisted of conjoint interviews, direct behavioral observations, and completion of the behavioral rating scales.

Observations by Sherry's mother, teacher, and an independent observer at both follow-up probes revealed maintenance of Sherry's increased initiations toward peers. Likewise, her mother and teacher provided several examples regarding Sherry's comfort in social interactions and outward desire to participate voluntarily in social activities.

The SSRS-P, SSRS-T, and SPPC were readministered at the 4-month follow-up. Across all rating scales, increases were noted on subscales of items assessing social initiation and social acceptance, as compared to ratings made prior to initiation of conjoint consultation services. In fact, ratings made by Sherry on the SPPC and Sherry's teacher on the SSRS-T after 4 months were higher than those made at the 9-day follow-up.

Social Validity

Social validity was assessed by both subjective evaluation and social comparison methods (Kazdin, 1977). Subjective evaluations involved global ratings and verbal statements of Sherry's social behaviors by her mother and teacher prior to and following treatment. Social comparison was assessed through direct observations of a nonwithdrawn peer, matched on gender, classroom, and approximate level of academic functioning. As depicted in Fig. 6.1, Sherry's social initiation behaviors increased to a level equal to or greater than her matched peer throughout the course of treatment. These gains were maintained at both follow-up probes.

Treatment Integrity

The integrity with which the behavioral programs were administered by consultees was assessed through self-monitoring (Gresham, 1989). Self-report rating scales were developed and completed by Sherry's mother and teacher, with high levels of adherence to treatment procedures noted by both. Specifically, Sherry's teacher reported 100% adherence to all treatment components on all days of treatment. Her mother reported a range of 89–100% adherence, with an average of 94% across all treatment days. Informal observations, interview data, and behavioral records also suggested adherence to the treatment programs.

Case Discussion

The case of Sherry demonstrated several important components of consultation. First, several assessment methods were used to obtain a comprehensive account of Sherry's withdrawn behaviors. Information gleaned in the CPII and the direct observations yielded important information regarding the severity of her social withdrawal, as well as conditions that might have contributed to it. Especially noteworthy was her mother's observation regarding Sherry's brother's behaviors, specifically his propensity to respond for Sherry in ways that allowed her to avoid social interaction.

A second noteworthy feature of this case study involved the various procedures by which treatment effectiveness was assessed. Specifically, direct objective data were considered the primary outcome measure; however, other important indices such as social validity, treatment acceptability, and treatment integrity were also assessed. Third, a carefully conducted AB design was instituted, incorporating many procedures recommended by Kratochwill (1985). Because of its thoroughness in assessing outcome and evaluating consultation efficacy, this case served as a template for those that follow.

Third, a particularly positive aspect of this case study involved the relationship that was formed between Sherry's mother and her teacher. Specifically, as the consultation process and interviews progressed, many instances arose wherein the consultees began conversing among themselves. They began sharing comments and observations about Sherry's behaviors and progress and reinforced each other frequently. On several occasions, they reported pleasure with the consultation procedures and indicated that they would like to continue communicating about Sherry's performance even after consultation ended. There is reason to believe that in this case, the CBC procedures fostered positive relations between Sherry's mother and her teacher.

IRRATIONAL FEARS: THE CASE OF MARK

Susan Sheridan and Denise Colton

Background Information

The child in this case was "Mark," a 6-year-old boy referred for consultation by his kindergarten teacher for repeated exaggerated and highly emotional reports of "monsters" and spiders in his room. His teacher discussed his apparent overactive imagination with his mother who reported that because he actually believed that such creatures were physically present in his bedroom, he slept on the floor of his parents' room. Together, the teacher and his parent agreed to discuss the situation with a school psychologist consultant.

The case study was conducted in a suburban city. Consultation was initiated at the end of the school year. The Conjoint Problem Identification Interview (CPII) was conducted at the child's private school. Because the school year concluded prior to completion of consultation, the Conjoint Problem Analysis Interview (CPAI) and Conjoint Treatment Evaluation Interview (CTEI) were conducted at the teacher's home.

Problem Identification

The problem identification phase of CBC was initiated to (1) review general characteristics that might be related to Mark's difficulties sleeping in his own room, (2) rule out possible interfering medical problems, (3) identify the specific concern of Mark's mother and teacher, (4) generate a consultation/intervention goal, and (5) develop baseline data collection procedures. Problem identification entailed completion of parent and teacher rating scales (i.e., Child Behavior Checklist [CBCL], Achenbach, 1991a; Teacher's Report Form [TRF], Achenbach, 1991b) and a CPII.

Mark's mother and teacher completed the CBCL and TRF, respectively. All T-scores were within the average range (Internalizing scores were 52 and 59; Externalizing scores were 41 and 49 for the parent and teacher forms, respectively). Factor scores also revealed no significant concerns, with T-scores ranging from 55 to 68 on the CBCL and from 55 to 63 on the TRF. Items rated by Mark's mother as very true included "Can't get his mind off certain thoughts [monsters]," "Fears certain situations [going to bed alone at night]," "Nightmares," and other problems ("Has had night terrors"). Items rated by Mark's teacher as very true were "Fears certain situations [sleeping in his own bedroom]," "Worrying," and "Talks out of turn."

The consultant met with Mark's mother and his teacher for approximately 1 hour for a CPII. Both consultees indicated that Mark seemed to demonstrate a "genuine" fear of monsters and spiders in his room. Behavioral manifestations of this fear included setting elaborate traps to "catch" the monsters, crying to the point of physical illness when forced to sleep in his room, reporting detailed stories at school of "something" grabbing his ankle from under the bed, and sleeping on the floor of his parents' room. During this interview, the goal target behavior was operationalized as "going to bed and sleeping in his bed the entire night." The problem was reported to be in the setting of his own house only (he slept appropriately at his grandparents' house and in his own bedroom in his family's previous house). He also took naps appropriately during the daytime hours in his own bedroom. Previous attempts to resolve the problem included allowing Mark to sleep in his brother's room, using a star chart, and reading to Mark until he fell asleep. These programs met with partial success but were followed inconsistently by his parents. It was reported that Mark had prior sleeping difficulties that had subsided, including enuresis until 5 1/2 years of age and periodic night terrors that occurred over approximately 4 years.

A data collection procedure was developed for Mark's mother to document conditions surrounding the nighttime and sleep routines. Specifically, a "sleep log" was developed on which Mark's mother recorded his assigned and actual bedtimes, length of time in bed, emotional state when going to bed, activities from dinner to bedtime, topics of discussion at bedtime, activities once in bed, and occurrence of sleep problems and means of resolution. Mark's mother was asked to keep this record for 2 weeks, at which time the consultant would reconvene with her and the teacher for purposes of a CPAI.

Following is an excerpt from the CPII illustrating the discussion of Mark's mother's and teacher's concerns and the process of narrowing in on a behavioral target that is manageable and measurable.

Consultant: What are some of the things that you're concerned about?

Parent: Well, actually, the only thing that I'm concerned about with Mark is the fact that he does not like or want to go to bed in his own room by himself at night.

Consultant: Mm hmm.

Parent: As I've told his teacher, he seems to have a genuine fear of something or someone, you know, mosters, I mean. He has even rigged up these elaborate traps in his room.

Consultant: Mm hmm.

Parent: You know, string going all over the place to catch the monsters.

Consultant: Mm.

Parent: That really is my only concern with him, and...

Teacher: He actually told me that one time that something actually grabbed his ankle from under the bed.

Parent: Oh.

Teacher: That he knew it was real because it grabbed him and it wasn't, he said, "It's not my imagination, something grabbed me."

Parent: Really?

Teacher: Yeah.

Parent: I, I just, I don't know what to do. I've done all kinds of things, you know...we've had our little chart, and, "Gee, if you go to bed tonight and sleep in your bed...all night, if you stay there..."

Consultant: Mm hmm. Mm hmm.

Parent: "...you get up in the morning, then you'll get a star and if you get...." You know, first we start out with just one day at a time, okay, if he did it for that night he got a star, or...something special that night, okay, then we try two days and then we try three days...

Consultant: Mm hmm.

Parent: ...and after a week, you know, he'd get something special but it never got to a week.

Consultant: Mm hmm. How far did you get with him?

Parent: Oh, I don't remember, I think we got four or five days...I think we got like five days, and then probably what happened was the weekend came and we are much less structured on the week-end.... On the weekend we just kind of, you know, hang loose and we don't have a set bedtime and things like that. And then that maybe broke the cycle. But like I say, he seems to have a genuine fear.

Later in interview:

Consultant: Okay, another example [of irrational fears] is that he sets traps in his room to catch the monster?
Parent: Yes.
Consultant: And comes to school and talks about tarantulas?...
Parent: When it's a little spider.
Consultant: Okay. I guess there's a few different directions that we could go. One would be...it sounds like the bedtime routine is the one you're mostly concerned with.
Parent: Mm hmm. And then staying, you know, in bed, if he awakens at night....
Consultant: Okay, so staying in bed would be the goal that you might have.
Parent: Going to bed in his bed and staying there, yes.
Consultant: Okay. I think that would be a real manageable kind of thing to try to work out, because it's specific and we'd know if he's doing it or not...
Parent: Oh yes, yeah.
Consultant: So rather than trying to address this global kind of fear that he has...
Parent: Mm hmm.

Problem Analysis

The second stage of CBC (problem analysis) was initiated with the CPAI. This interview lasted approximately 1 1/2 hours and involved two phases (analysis and plan). The analysis phase involved inspecting baseline data and conducting strength and conditions analyses. During the 2- week baseline condition, Mark failed to sleep in his own bedroom on all nights. On 14 nights, he slept on the floor of his parents' room. A conditions analysis revealed no significant antecedents immediately preceding bedtime routines. The hours between the end of school and dinner were generally uneventful (e.g., Mark often played baseball, watched television, played outdoors). Between dinner and bedtime, the routine often included homework, a shower, stories, or television. Although no significant antecedents were identified that immediately preceded Mark's bedtime, his cognitive beliefs of monsters and spiders residing in his room were considered significant setting events that contributed to the occurrence of his bedtime difficulties.

Events while Mark was in bed, including conversations and behaviors, were analyzed as part of a situational analysis. The content of discussions in which Mark engaged at bedtime included "Teenage Mutant Ninja Turtles," murderers, baseball, classmates, and difficulties falling asleep. Some nights Mark watched television or read magazines at bedtime. On one occasion, he asked to sleep in his parents' bed. This request was declined and Mark was instructed to sleep in his own bed. Mark failed to comply with this instruction with no apparent consequences. On all other nights, Mark was allowed to sleep on the floor of his parents' bedroom with no conflict.

During the plan phase, a program was developed to increase Mark's behavior of sleeping in his own room. It was believed that Mark's difficulty sleeping in his own room stemmed from a cognitively based setting event (irrational fear) that was reinforced by his parents, who allowed him to sleep in their bedroom. Because his fears appeared to be very pervasive, a gradual fading-of-environment procedure was deemed necessary. Likewise, because previous efforts were only partially successful, firm and consistent contingencies were established and identified as central to the potential success of the program.

Following is a sample from the CPAI. This excerpt first illustrates the consultant's efforts to stay focused on a behavioral target. Second, the integration of important treatment components in plan development is highlighted.

Consultant: And at this point, I would like to go from the assumption that it's really just irrational fear.
Parent: Mm hmm.
Consultant: And we talked last week about different ways we can address that, either by trying to address the fear aspect of it...
Parent: Mm hmm.
Consultant: ...or by helping...by coming from the other direction and addressing the behavior, the behavioral aspect of it...
Parent: Mm hmm.
Consultant: ...and focusing on trying to get him to alter his behavior and to go to bed. Hopefully that will indirectly address the fear.
Parent: Right.
Consultant: I still think that's probably the best way to go.
Parent: Okay.

Later in interview:

Consultant: I think everything we do is going to require some limits and rules.

Parent: Right. Mm hmm.

Consultant: Related to this is consistency.

Parent: Right.

Consultant: That means every night.

Parent: Mm hmm.

Consultant: That means mom and dad, and his brother for that matter.

Parent: Right, yes, yes.

Consultant: It's not just you and Mark.

Parent: Right.

Consultant: And one other thing that we've talked about was gradually fading.... Where are the rooms situated?

Parent: Very close proximity, we have a very small house. Very close proximity. We're all, you know, we're all just right...

Consultant: So maybe two or three steps difference?

Parent: Oh maybe five, from Mark's room to ours. It's not very far. And his brother's is just...here's his door and here's our door.

Consultant: Okay, and your goal is to get him into his own room?

Parent: Unless his brother would be willing to switch beds...although I almost think if we're going to do it, he needs to get used to the room he's going to be sleeping in.

Consultant: Mm hmm. This fading him to go back to his own room...it's really just another step or two. This could be one of the high points. He might have...

Parent: A pit stop?

Consultant: Well, you might...he'd earn smaller reinforcers.

Parent: Right.

Consultant: Or smaller steps like being half way between your bed and the door. And then another one for being in the doorway, but a bigger one for being in the hallway. And then another smaller one for being...

Parent: A little further down the hall.

Consultant: A little further, but a bigger one, his brother's room could be one of the hurdles.

Parent: Okay. One of the bigger ones.

> Consultant: And his room could be the biggest.... So, three components: fading, self-monitoring, and some kind of visible reinforcement...
> Parent: Yeah, I like that. What do you think?
> Teacher: That sounds good.
> Consultant: I think it sounds very good.
> Teacher: That sounds like something Mark can live with too.

Treatment (Plan) Implementation

The intervention was implemented by Mark's parents. In the fading technique, Mark was gradually moved to his own bed in small, graded steps. Specifically, five equidistant steps were identified that represented small progressions from Mark's parents' room to his own bed. During the implementation of the program, Mark added two additional steps to further ease the transition.

The intervention was implemented for 15 consecutive nights. Mark's mother designed a gamelike chart depicting a ladder with "bases" representing each step. Two rungs separated each base to represent the criterion of two successful nights at each step. "Home plate" was depicted at the top of the ladder, representing a "home run" when he reached his own bed. Successful performance each night (i.e., sleeping all night in the defined physical space) was reinforced by coloring a ladder rung on the chart. "Mastery" (defined as two consecutive successful nights) at each step was required before moving to the next designated step. When two rungs were colored in (representing successful performance for two nights at the same step), a reinforcer of Mark's choice (e.g., a folder, playing with dad, baseball cards) was provided. A long-term secondary reinforcer (i.e., a life-size Michael Jordan poster) was provided for sleeping an entire night in his own bed.

When his parents attempted to present the program to Mark, he initially resisted (i.e., he refused to discuss the program with his parents). With some prompting, he reviewed the program with his parents and assisted in the establishment of a reinforcement menu. Likewise, each night Mark asked to return to a prior step. However, Mark's mother reported that she remained very firm and consistent and did not allow such regression to occur.

Treatment (Plan) Evaluation

A CTEI with the consultant and Mark's mother and teacher was conducted in the home of Mark's teacher 15 days following the initiation of the

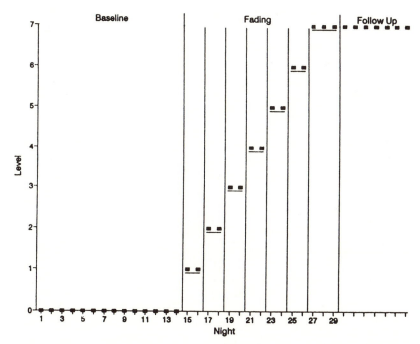

Figure 6.2. Number of consecutive nights Mark slept in locations (levels) of increasing difficulty, gradually reaching the target of his own bed. (*Source:* Sheridan, S. M., & Colton, D. L. [1994]. Conjoint behavioral consultation: A review and case study. *Journal of Educational and Psychological Consultation*, *5*, 211–228. Reprinted with permission.)

fading procedure. An AB design with follow-up was used to evaluate the treatment effects in this case. The results of treatment are presented in Figure 6.2. Two weeks of baseline data collection by Mark's mother showed 0 occasions of sleeping in own room and 14 occasions of sleeping on floor of parents' room. As can be seen in Figure 6.2, Mark demonstrated an immediate response to treatment, with perfect performance at each criterion level. During the 2 weeks of intervention, he slept each night in the location predefined in consultation. Given that the goal of consultation had been met, procedures for maintenance and generalization were established. Specifically, it was decided that nightly reinforcers would continue for 1 week, with gradual fading of reinforcers after that time. The reinforcement schedule was modified from continuous to twice weekly, once weekly, and finally faded completely.

The consultant contacted Mark's mother 1 month following the termination of consultation for a follow-up assessment. Mark's mother reported that he continued to sleep in his own bed and demonstrated no regression at any time.

In the following CTEI excerpt, the consultant and consultees discuss perceptions of the intervention (social validity), and specific behavioral data attesting to goal attainment.

Consultant: Is he pretty proud of himself, that he can do this and...

Parent: Well, I don't know, it's interesting because the first night I said, "Oh, you should feel so proud of yourself," and he says, "Why?" I said, "Because you've accomplished something."

Consultant: It was hard for him.

Parent: Yeah. "You know, this has been, this has been hard for you and it's something you've accomplished and you should be proud of yourself." And then that night when his dad got home, he said, "Dad, do you want to see my Michael Jordan poster?" Because his reward was a Michael Jordan poster. Michael Jordan, eight feet in the air, and ah, so his dad said, "Oh, you slept in your bed, you should be so proud of yourself!" And he said "I am!"

Consultant: That's great.

Later in interview:

Parent: So anyway, it's worked well. I mean, almost each night he has asked if he could either move back a step or sleep in our room or something, he's always asked, but when I have said, "No, you know you can't spend more than two nights in a spot," or "No, go sleep in your bed," it hasn't been a problem. He said, "Okay."

Consultant: Mm hmm. So he's still asking even though he's in his own bed?

Parent: Mm hmm. Mm hmm.

Consultant: But you're being real firm, and matter-of-fact.

Parent: Mm hmm. And so far it's working.

Consultant: Well good, good.

Teacher: Maybe he's comfortable, or getting comfortable, in knowing that there's not monsters there.

Parent: Well, and I asked him too, I said, "Isn't it comfortable sleeping in bed, wasn't that nice to sleep in your bed?" And he said, "Yeah, it was real nice for my back." (Laughs)

Consultant: Can we say that our goal, the initial goal that we talked about was having Mark sleeping in his own bed...all night long...do you think we met that goal?

Parent: Absolutely.

Consultant: Great!

—————————————————————————————————— Case Discussion

This case depicts the use of CBC with a unique and rather uncommon behavioral problem. Specifically, the procedures were used to extinguish irrational fears of spiders and monsters in the bedroom of a kindergarten student. The fears were exhibited at school only; however related behavioral manifestations were evident at school (i.e., exaggerated stories about the monsters and spiders in his bedroom) that may have affected his school performance.

Results of this case study were positive and substantial. Perhaps more than the other case studies presented here, the behavioral outcome in this case was immediate, stable, and long-lasting. It is believed that the potency of the intervention, developed collaboratively by Mark's parent, teacher, and the consultant, produced this strong effect.

—————————————— ACADEMIC UNDERACHIEVEMENT: THE CASE OF JANE

JoAnn Galloway and Susan Sheridan

—————————————————————————————— Background Information

The child in this case was "Jane,"an 8-year-old girl referred for consultation by her 3rd-grade teacher for consistently failing to complete assigned homework in math. When work was turned in, Jane's accuracy rates were often below 70%. Further, her performance pattern was quite inconsistent. On some days, Jane completed her work and obtained a high degree of accuracy; on others, she completed no work and thus received very poor performance grades. Jane's teacher had tried various interventions previously to increase Jane's completion and accuracy rates; however, these interventions resulted in continued inconsistent performance. Her mother was concerned with the inconsistencies in Jane's performance and agreed to work with the school psychologist consultant and Jane's teacher to identify the specific problem and develop an intervention to address the concern.

The case study was conducted in a suburban city. Consultation was initiated during the second half of the school year. The Conjoint Problem Identification Interview (CPII) was conducted at public elementary school. All interviews were conducted in the office of the school psychologist.

Problem Identification

Several methods were used to define and assess the specific target behavior to be addressed in consultation. These methods included conjoint interviews with Jane's teacher and mother, analysis of her math assignment sheets, and the Conners Teacher Questionnaire (Conners, 1990). Further, an intellectual screening measure (Kaufman Brief Intelligence Test [KBIT]) (Kaufman & Kaufman, 1990) and academic assessment (Woodcock-Johnson Test of Achievement) (Woodcock & Mather, 1990) were included to rule out a learning disability.

On the KBIT, Jane achieved an overall Composite score of 108, with a Vocabulary score of 100 and a Matrices score of 114 (mean of KBIT = 100; SD = 15), suggesting intellectual abilities in the average range. She earned grade equivalents of 4.7 and 5.4 on the Woodcock-Johnson Math subtests of Calculation and Applied Problems, respectively. These were both above her 3rd-grade placement and discredited the existence of a learning disability. The Hyperactivity Index of the Conners Teacher Questionnaire yielded a T-score of 69 (mean = 50; SD = 10).

The consultant met with Jane's mother and teacher for approximately 1 hour for a CPII. Both consultees indicated that Jane had difficulty staying focused and on task when engaged in activities. She was described by the consultees as both internally and externally distractible. For example, her mother reported that her own thoughts seemed to distract her; her teacher added that peers, objects, and "something going wrong" (e.g., glue cap getting stuck on the bottle) caused great difficulty attending to tasks. Her teacher commented that Jane often had difficulty starting, continuing, and completing tasks, including academic work. She also had difficulty with tasks requiring organization, such as preparing for the beginning of school and returning home. Similarly, her mother agreed that she had a hard time preparing for school and bed and completing chores around the house. Following an extensive discussion of problematic behaviors, Jane's mother and teacher (with the assistance of the consultant) determined that her difficulty staying on task resulted in lack of work completion and poor academic grades. Problems in the area of math were identified as a priority, since this subject area required products on an almost daily basis (such as worksheets). Hence, work completion and accuracy were prioritized for consultation.

A tentative conditional analysis was conducted to evaluate factors surrounding Jane's difficulty completing assignments and maintaining an acceptable accuracy level. The environmental conditions surrounding her difficulties were thus explored. At school, her teacher generally provided verbal instructions regarding how to initiate and complete the task. She rarely started her work immediately; once started, she was often distracted to the point that she failed to complete assignments. As a consequence, she typically remained in the classroom during recess or other enjoyable activities to complete her work. Because this practice failed to ensure work completion, she was required to take her work home with her as homework. Jane's mother reported that at home, conflicts often arose as she attempted to encourage Jane to complete her homework. The difficulty completing her homework after school in the home setting was compounded by the fact that Jane also failed to complete household chores; this failure resulted in difficulties for Jane's mother and for the relationship between Jane and her mother.

A behavioral goal was established by Jane's mother and teacher during the CPII. Specifically, they believed that Jane was currently completing approximately 33% of her math work and that 80-85% would be a desirable level for both completion and accuracy. Baseline data collection procedures were established, which involved daily collection and scoring of math assignments by the teacher and consultant. Percentages of work completion and accuracy were recorded on a daily basis.

Selected excerpts from the CPII follow:

Teacher: In dealing with Jane in the classroom, she takes a very long time to complete any task, has a hard time staying on task, um, is distracted easily. Um, not only by her peers, but by little things that may not be going as smoothly as she thinks they ought to. Ah, such as, an example, the glue bottle...one day she spent 45 minutes trying to figure out the cap of the glue bottle. And I spoke to her to get another glue bottle, ah, but she was into discovering why it was not working, figuring it out, and so from that point on, she was very involved in her own little world and the art project went undone. Or she ended up taking it home. But not only in art or, I just see this same type of behavior...she'll know what to do, but she may get distracted by drawing something on the paper or by, um, you know, doing her flash, or her times tables around the edge of the paper or, you know, some distraction that keeps her from being on task.

Consultant: Okay, okay, how about home?

Parent: There is some, um, the distractibility, even just something that just goes through her mind will, will distract her...something that has nothing to do with what she's doing. Just a certain thought or something like that. It's very hard to get her to sit down and finish her homework, to actually have her sit and do it. Um, she's been there for hours at work...she gets distracted by every little thing.

Later in interview:

Consultant: Well, we've been talking about the behavior setting where she does the behavior and you, and you really both said that it occurs a, across just about everything you ask her to do. Whether it's getting her backpack ready for school in the morning, changing from her shoes to her boots, um, getting the math test done, getting something done at home. At school, what's the most problematic time that it occurs, or situation that it occurs?

Teacher: Um, when she is doing her art work, she's in her own little world and if she enjoys that so much, I think that that's a time for her to express her creativity. And boy, she can do, ah, in a couple of art projects that we've done, she's done detail on, you know, the material of the people that she's drawing picture on, to the point where, you know, three weeks from now we could still be doing the same picture!

Consultant: So does she carry it over then into other academic times when she should be doing other things?

Teacher: Mm hmm. And then her desk is very cluttered. Her, her organizational skills...I mean, she just doesn't use them.

Parent: Mm hmm, and then it's too overwhelming to do anything about it?

Teacher: Yes, exactly. And she becomes overwhelmed and then at the end of the day she has a real stack. And then if I say, "Jeez, let's get that one done and get that turned in," she gets a little huffy, you know, she doesn't...

Consultant: Well, that might be a clue though...she gets a lot of papers in front of her and she gets lost in the detail and can't figure out where to start.

Teacher: When she gets backed up, you know...

Parent: Mm hmm.

Teacher: ... After the, you know, or after the hour...say, we've done reading; she still may not have her vocabulary done or her comprehension work done...

Consultant: Mm hmm.

Teacher: ... And so I'll ask her to put it to the side and we start our math, and so she's not behind on her math instruction and so she understands her paper...

Parent: But she still has that reading paper?

Teacher: But she still has her reading, and then, you know, and then she doesn't do her math, so then it gets piled there and then when I have a finish time, you know, such as a story or something that she can work on, then she's kind of got it everywhere...

Consultant: Mm hmm.

Teacher: So she's not sure where...I think it becomes a real organizational task for her.

Consultant: So then not only does she have the issue of not getting the work done, but she has the issue of sorting through the papers and figuring out where to start...

Later in interview:

Consultant: Okay. What would be acceptable, what would we think that would be okay, what would we be happy with if she were to do it, given that she's done, instead of a half, third to a half. What do most of your kids do?

Teacher: I would want 80% done.

Consultant: Okay, how about you, how do you feel about that?

Parent: I think that would maybe be fair, by taking into consideration that I don't always do 100%!

Consultant: So if we can pick it up from 50% to 85%.

Problem Analysis

Approximately 1 week following the CPII, Jane's mother, teacher, and consultant convened for a Conjoint Problem Analysis Interview (CPAI). A review of the baseline data indicated that Jane completed an average of 35.5% of her work (range = 14-100%), with a great deal of variability in her work. Her accuracy rates ranged from 8% to 100%, with a mean of 26.5%. On the second day of baseline data collection, she completed 100% of her work with 100% accuracy. It was speculated that this result may have been due to the fact that the assignments were now being collected by her teacher, which was not a typical practice.

A skills analysis was conducted to assess the degree to which Jane possessed the prerequisite skills to complete math assignments accurately. A review of her math worksheets revealed that the problems that Jane attempted to complete were typically completed accurately, suggesting that she understood the necessary math concepts and processes. Environmental conditions surrounding Jane's lack of work completion were also explored with her mother and teacher. Her mother and teacher both noted that Jane's behaviors may have been related to her affect and attitude when she arrived at school. Specifically, when she had a difficult morning at home and arrived at school in a bad mood, her behaviors were generally problematic. Further, students' desks were arranged in a table format that required her to face three other children with many objects on top of her desk. These conditions may have contributed to her distractiblity.

A unique aspect of this case was the inclusion of Jane in the CPAI and CTEI. Thus, she was able to contribute directly in the development of an intervention and selection of reinforcers. The central feature of the intervention was a home-note procedure (see Figure 6.3). Jane was provided with a home note on which five specific behaviors related to work skills and task completion were listed. Jane kept the note on her desk to serve as a reminder of important academic behaviors. During each math period, her teacher recorded on the note itself whether or not Jane completed each behavior. Jane took the note home and was responsible for showing it to her mother, who reviewed her daily behaviors and math performance. A home-note manual was also provided to Jane's mother and teacher, which outlined the rationale for home notes, reviewed procedures for developing home notes, provided instructions on dealing with implementation problems, made suggestions for increasing their effectiveness, and listed ideas for reinforcers.

Jane, her mother, and her teacher decided that she would earn a reinforcer (chosen from a "grab bag") each day that 80% of her work was completed with at least 80% accuracy.

Additional features of the intervention were included as a function of contributing environmental factors identified during problem analysis. Specifically, Jane's mother reported that she would make efforts to arrange morning conditions at home to ensure that Jane arrived at school with a positive affect and attitude. Her teacher agreed to remove distractions from her desk and replace them with the one-sheet home note. Even Jane commented that she might find it useful to move to an alternative table apart from

My Daily Home Note

Name: _____ Week of: _____

	MON	TUE	WED	THUR	FRI
PAPER & PENCIL READY					
START WORKING RIGHT AWAY					
WORK UNTIL THE JOB IS FINISHED					
DO THE MATH CORRECTLY (80% OR BETTER)					
HAND THE WORK IN					

Comments: Mon. _____

Comments: Tues. _____

Comments: Wed. _____

Comments: Thurs. _____

Comments: Fri. _____

PARENT CHECKLIST

	MON	TUES	WED	THUR	FRI
I looked at the checklist.					
I praised my child for good work.					
I provided the agreed upon reward.					

Figure 6.3. Home note used with Jane.

the other students if she was experiencing difficulties with concentration and work completion. Jane's teacher agreed to continue to collect her math sheets each day and record completion and accuracy rates.

The following excerpts from the CPAI illustrate the role that Jane played in plan development:

Consultant: We talked about the things that happen before, before you have trouble getting your math done.

Jane: Mm hmm.

Consultant: Like you get interested in something else, or you have a lot to do at one time, and what happens afterwards is you have to stay in from fun things and take it home and get zeros and stuff like that. Have you noticed any patterns in, in how Jane does her math? Like, days when she tends to do better, people she's sitting by that she tends to do better, types of assignments? Anything like that?

Teacher: Sometimes it depends on what we've been reading, if she's really excited about what we're doing in reading, then it's hard to get off reading and go to math.

Consultant: Okay.

Teacher: When she first arrived at our classroom, some days were better days than other days and she seemed to be happy about coming and some days not to be too happy, and I think that affected her schoolwork.

Later in interview:

Consultant: Is there anything else that we can think of that's related to this? Anything else that we haven't already talked about that makes it hard for you to get your math done? Why do you think it's hard for you? Do you kind of get distracted by other things around you, maybe, other kids or other jobs?

Jane: Well, I don't know.

Consultant: Kind of hard to say. Anybody else have any ideas about why, what the behavior's related to? We've already talked about some things...attitude, amount of work to do...

Parent: Organization.

Consultant: ... organization skills.

Parent: Focusing on the task.

Consultant: Staying focused and organization, because those might be two things we can work on.

Later in interview:

Consultant: And, and we're just starting with math right now, but it has some organization things on it that we want you to practice doing. One of them is, having your paper and pencil ready at the start of math.

Jane: Mm hmm.

Consultant: Okay, and that means nothing else on the desk, just paper and pencil. When it's time to get started, to get started right away. Okay? To work until the job is finished. To work until...you have the amount Mrs. C. said "Check with me after you get this done." Instead of talking to somebody else or getting in your tote tray to look for something. Okay? And then do the work correctly, at least 80%. Okay? And hand the work in and Mrs. C. will check it off.

Teacher: I will just initial every day?

Consultant: Mm hmm, mm hmm.

Teacher: Okay.

Consultant: These things every day and only for math.

Teacher: Okay.

Consultant: And I've got a comment section here that you can use for anything that you want to communicate to each other. And then down here is the parent checklist, have to make sure that, um, you're looking at the checklist every day. That you're, um, praising Jane for the good work that she's doing. And that you provide whatever you agreed on as a home reward for doing this contract. Okay? Now, ideas for the home reward is something that I put together here. This is a manual that I put together, I copied some pictures, these aren't my own drawings, they're somebody else's. One thing about this sheet, though, is you have to make sure you have one every day.

Jane: I have to bring it back every day?

Consultant: Mm hmm, and your teacher fills it out and your mom looks at it and then you bring it back to your teacher for the next day.

Parent: Goes home every day and goes back to school every day.

Consultant: Mm hmm, yeah, that's a great idea. Okay, then, this gives an idea of how to start the home notes and some kinds of problems that sometimes happen with home notes and how to deal with them, and some ideas to make it fun, like using spinners with rewards or mystery motivators, or grab bags or saving up points that you might earn counting each one of these towards something that she might like to do. So, what we're going to do here is, let's make sure we got it. What's gonna, what's your desk gonna look like at math time?

Jane: Um, just paper and pencil out.

Consultant: Okay, good, and what, what are we going to do to help you get organized, what are you going to do after each little chunk of work that Mrs. C. says, "Get this piece done?... You only have this many minutes to do it."

Jane: Start on it right at that time.

Consultant: Start right away and keep working until when?

Jane: Till the end.

Consultant: Till the end of the time, then show it to Mrs. C. and she'll give you another little chunk to do, and that way, you're likely to get it all done in the time limit. And then when you bring that home, your mom and you are going to decide on some fun things that you can do at home as rewards, for really concentrating on doing well at math. Now we'll continue to keep track of your math performance so that we have that graph that I showed you before and what we're probably going to see is that your scores are going to be up here instead of down here.

Treatment Evaluation

Jane's math work completion and accuracy data continued to be collected during the treatment implementation stage using procedures identical to those used during baseline. Specifically, each math worksheet was collected at the end of each period; the number of problems completed was calculated, and percentage was determined by dividing this number by the number of items assigned. Items were then scored, and percentage accuracy was determined as the number of items correct divided by 100.

A Conjoint Treatment Evaluation Interview (CTEI) was conducted after 3 full days of treatment (see Figure 6.4). Jane met the performance criteria of 80% complete and accurate the first 2 days of treatment. On Day 3, however, she reverted to baseline levels (30% completed and 30% accurate). In discussing conditions surrounding this performance drop, confusion about criteria for positive reinforcement was discovered. Specifically, although Jane met the criteria of 80% completion and accuracy in math each day, her mother failed to deliver the reinforcer because not all performance cues (as indicated on her home note) were demonstrated. As a result, Jane refused

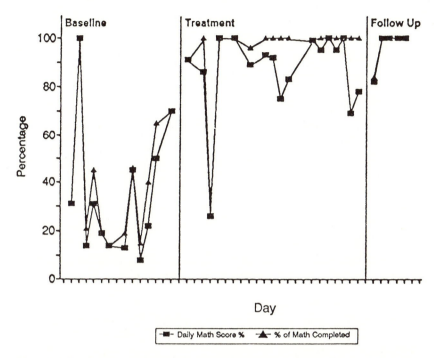

Figure 6.4. Jane's math completion and accuracy data across conditions. (*Source*: Galloway, J., & Sheridan, S. M. [1994]. Implementing scientific practices through case studies: Examples using home-school interventions and consultation. *Journal of School Psychology, 32*, 385–413. Reproduced with permission.)

to cooperate with the program on the 3rd day of treatment. This appeared to have resulted from a misunderstanding on the part of Jane, her mother, and her teacher regarding the criteria for earning the reward. The misunderstanding was discussed during the CTEI, and all agreed that Jane was able to demonstrate the required performance behaviors in addition to receiving at least 80% accuracy scores. Once the criteria for reinforcement were clarified (i.e., meet all performance criteria in addition to completing 80% of her math work at 80% accuracy), Jane's performance improved again and was generally stable throughout the remainder of the treatment and follow-up phases. A review of the intervention data indicated that Jane completed an average of 94.8% of her work with an average of 86.5% accuracy. At follow-up, Jane achieved a completion average of 96.8% and an accuracy average of 96.2%.

Following are brief excerpts from the CTEI:

Consultant: How have you felt about how she's done this week in comparison to other weeks?

Teacher: The first of the week was real good.

Jane: Mm hmm.

Teacher: She did pretty good. We had one area where she dropped down.

Jane: Mm hmm. I only have one sad face and a couple of straight.

Consultant: Mm hmm.

Teacher: Then one day we didn't get the note here and so then we got a sad face there...we didn't do as well that day...I think we were maybe not feeling real good about it.

Jane: Mm hmm. I thought mom said that I have to have all smiley faces.

Teacher: That's right...this whole day.

Parent: The whole day, huh.

Jane: Then I'm...oh I goofed.... Now what am I going to do? I mean there's no chance...I'm trying to get smiley faces and she said, "Well, then we'll do one, then we'll try one day and if you get all smiley faces, then you might get to put your hand in the grab..."

Parent: If you get all smiley faces one day, you get your hand in the grab bag.

Consultant: Mm hmm.

Parent: And that can happen each day.

Jane: Mm hmm.

Consultant: Like today you're going to do it, right? You've got all smiley faces and you got 100%. That is wonderful. We've had a little problem getting going, but even with the problems we've had, out of the five days...four out of the five, you got at least 80% or better on your math.

Teacher: Mm hmm.

Jane: Mm hmm.

Consultant: Which is wonderful, wonderful. Now you may not have gotten all those smiley faces, but you did improve a lot in math. And the reason for those other things Jane, is to help you get a good score on your math, and also to teach you how to...the kinds of school behaviors that make you get good scores on things, that's why they're important. Okay?

Jane: Mm hmm.

Consultant: What should we do to make sure that we keep on getting good days like we've had today?

Jane: Um...remember to have everything, just have the desk looking nice while you're doing math.

Consultant: Mm hmm.

Jane: And work right when I get the paper.

Consultant: Mm hmm.

Teacher: Good job.

Consultant: Does that sound good?

Teacher: Mm hmm.

Consultant: So mainly keep going with the same plan. Is the reward system working okay?

Parent: We don't know yet.

Consultant: Oh, we only had it one day, but what I'm wondering is to have the all-or-nothing kind of thing where she has to have all of...

Parent: It seems to provide...

Consultant: So it's not too tough to only get the reward if you get perfect, do you think?

Teacher: It's not too tough.

Consultant: Okay, so we don't need to change the plan. We just need to work on it longer. That means you've got to do all of those things besides getting 80% on your math, to get the grab bag, okay? But we know you can do it because you did it perfectly today. Okay, so we're going to keep on going and could we just wait a couple of weeks before we check again to make sure that everything's going okay?

The identification of conditions surrounding Jane's drop in performance early in treatment was crucial to the remainder of the implementation stage; thus, the involvement of her mother in a structured consultation approach was highlighted. In this case, the use of a home note in isolation (without the supportive consultation sessions) may have resulted in treatment failure.

The Conners Teacher Questionnaire was readministered at the time of treatment evaluation. On the readministration, Jane received a Hyperactivity Index T-score of 57. This represented an improvement of slightly more than one standard deviation from her pretest score and placed her behaviors within the average range.

Treatment Acceptability

The degree to which Jane, her mother, and her teacher found the consultation/home-note procedures acceptable was assessed using the Behavior Intervention Rating Scale (BIRS) (Von Brock & Elliott, 1987; Elliott & Von

Brock Treuting, 1991) and the Children's Intervention Rating Profile (CIRP) (Witt & Elliott, 1985).

The BIRS was administered to Jane's mother and teacher to assess their perception of the acceptability of CBC. The BIRS is a 24-item instrument that assesses the degree to which consumers of treatment view the procedures as acceptable, effective, and efficient. Each item is scored on a 6-point Likert scale, with 1 indicating strong disagreement and 6 indicating strong agreement. The mean item scores were 4.96 and 5.63 for Jane's mother and teacher, respectively. These scores suggest that each consultee perceived the conjoint consultation/home-note procedures to be very acceptable. Jane's teacher rated almost all items with a 6 (highly acceptable). Among the items her mother rated with a 6 were "Overall, I believe the procedures were beneficial" and "I would feel comfortable recommending the use of these procedures to other parents."

The CIRP is a 7-item scale on which students report the degree to which they find intervention procedures to be acceptable. Each item is scored on a 5-point Likert scale, with 1 representing strong disagreement and 5 representing strong agreement. On the CIRP, Jane's mean item score of 4.0 suggests that she perceived the intervention favorably.

Social Validity

Social validity (the clinical meaningfulness of the behavior change) (Kazdin, 1977) was assessed in two ways. The first form, *subjective evaluation*, involved assessing the consultees' perceptions of Jane's behaviors following treatment. Two items from the BIRS (i.e., "The intervention proved effective in changing the child's problem behavior" and "The intervention quickly improved the child's behavior") were considered for purposes of social validity. Jane's teacher provided a score of 6 for each item, indicating strong agreement. Her mother provided scores of 5 and 4, respectively for the items. These scores suggested agreement with the items, but not at the same magnitude as the teacher. On open-ended questions, Jane's teacher reported that "the intervention helped Jane's performance to improve to better than adequate" and that "this intervention was very successful in improving both completion of work and accuracy."

A second form of social validity was *social comparison*. This method involved Jane's teacher collecting the math work of a comparison peer (deemed by Jane's teacher to be of average math ability) during treatment and comparing the peer's daily math performance to Jane's. The comparison peer obtained a mean daily math score of 73%, compared to Jane's mean accuracy score of 86.5%. This result suggests that Jane actually performed at a higher level during treatment than her comparison peer.

Treatment Integrity

Two forms of treatment integrity were assessed in the case study: integrity of the consultation procedures as implemented by the school psychologist and integrity of the intervention protocol as implemented by Jane's mother and teacher.

All of the CBC interviews were audiotaped. An individual not involved in the case study listened to the tapes and used the Consultation Objectives Checklist (Kratochwill & Bergan, 1990) to indicate each interview objective met by the consultant. In this case, the school psychologist-consultant met 86%, 92%, and 78% of the objectives for the CPII, CPAI, and CTEI, respectively.

The degree to which Jane's mother followed the home-note intervention procedures was assessed by self-report on the daily home note. Specifically, 3 items were included on the bottom of the note to assess whether the parent looked at the checklist, praised Jane's good work, and provided agreed-upon rewards. Across all treatment days, Jane's mother reported 100% adherence to the treatment procedures. Similarly, Jane's teacher was provided with a 6-item checklist of specific components of the intervention and indicated the intervention steps she performed daily. Across 19 days on which she provided self-monitoring data, Jane's teacher reported performing 94% of the treatment components.

Case Discussion

There are many components of this case study worthy of discussion. First, both consultees and Jane agreed that the procedures were helpful in assisting Jane to focus on her work, remain on task, and complete her math assignments accurately. Improvements were seen in the consistency with which she completed her work, which resulted in a concomitant improvement in her accuracy rates. Behaviors suggestive of attentional problems were also improved, as indicated on the Conners Teacher Questionnaire.

Some confusion regarding the criteria for the delivery of reinforcers became evident in an initial TEI session. The disagreement between Jane and her mother resulted in Jane's failure to participate in the program on one day and to complete her math work. The individualized consultation procedures provided an opportunity for the consultant to clarify the criteria for reinforcement immediately, which resulted in Jane's continued participation and subsequent stable performance. If there had been no such consultation it is possible that disagreements on the parameters for reinforcement would have continued and that Jane would have continued to demonstrate noncompliance.

An important aspect of this case study is highlighted by the fact that Jane's mother and teacher were provided with instructions for establishing and using home notes apart from consultation. Specifically, the home-note manual included procedural details regarding the use of home notes, with several suggestions on increasing the effectiveness of the program. Still, some confusion was evident and required individual consultation for clarification. It is possible that the consultation procedures, and the relationship that was formed, fostered communication and follow-through on the part of Jane's mother and teacher.

This case also illustrates the benefits of having the client involved in some aspects of the procedures. Specifically, Jane was asked to attend the sessions at the point at which the intervention was discussed. This approach was perceived as very desirable, in that Jane liked her ability to participate in the selection of reinforcers. She also stated that she might find it useful to move to a less distracting place in the classroom when she found it difficult to concentrate. It is likely that Jane felt ownership in the intervention, as she considered herself a part of its development, which may have added to its effectiveness. Jane also contributed in the CTEI, reporting that she saw the benefit of having her desk cleared off and starting tasks right away.

FAILING TO FOLLOW DIRECTIONS AND TANTRUMMING: THE CASE OF SUZANNE

Sherry Robertson

Background Information

Suzanne is a 4-year-old preschool student enrolled in a Head Start program. Suzanne's referral originated from her mother due to aggressive behaviors (i.e., hitting, kicking, material destruction) exhibited at home. At school, Suzanne's teacher reported that Suzanne did not exhibit aggressive behavior. However, her teacher did report that Suzanne had difficulty paying attention during large-group activities. Suzanne was referred for consultation, and both her teacher and her mother agreed to participate in conjoint consultation.

The problem-identification phase of the consultation process was initiated to (1) review the results of screening; (2) define the problem in behavioral terms; (3) examine the behavior in terms of antecedent, situation, and consequent conditions across settings; (4) discuss a goal for behavior change across settings; and (5) establish a procedure for the collection of baseline data across settings. Problem identification involved Suzanne's mother and teacher completing rating scales and a Conjoint Problem Identification Interview (CPII).

Suzanne's mother completed the parent version of the Social Skills Rating System (SSRS-P) and the parent form of the Child Behavior Checklist (CBCL). On the SSRS-P, Suzanne obtained a Social Skills score of 57 (mean = 100; SD = 15) and a Problem Behaviors score of 137. These scores suggested significant deficits in social skills and excesses in problem behaviors. On the Teacher Report form of the CBCL (CBCL-TRF), Suzanne's Total Scale score, Internalizing score, and Externalizing score were all in the clinical range. Suzanne's scores fell within the clinical range on the Withdrawn, Social Problems, Thought Problems, Attention Problems, Delinquent Behavior, and Aggressive Behavior subscales. Finally, she scored within the normal range on the Somatic Complaints and Anxious/Depressed subscales.

Suzanne's teacher completed the teacher version of the SSRS (SSRS-T) and the CBCL-TRF. On the SSRS-T, Suzanne received a Social Skills score of 83 and a Problem Behavior score of 114. On the CBCL-TRF, Suzanne's Total Scale T-Score, Internalizing T-Score, and externalizing T-Score were all in the normal range. Suzanne's scores fell within the borderline clinical range on the Thought Problems subscale. She scored in the normal range on the Withdrawn, Somatic Complaints, Anxious/Depressed, Social Problems, Attention Problems, Delinquent Behavior, and Aggressive Behavior subscales.

The consultant and Suzanne's mother and teacher met for approximately 1 hour for the CPII. During the CPII, it was determined that the initial focus for consultation in the home would be to increase Suzanne's appropriate behavior and decrease her aggressive behavior. Suzanne's mother identified hitting, kicking, and destructive acts toward material objects as the most troublesome behaviors. Thus, they were identified as the specific target behaviors at home. Suzanne's mother reported that Suzanne was often aggressive when given a directive or when she desired individual attention (e.g., when sisters came home from school). However, she also stated that Suzanne was sometimes aggressive for no apparent reason. Getting dressed in the morning and when her sisters returned home from school were the most difficult times for Suzanne, and her aggressive behavior often escalated during these times. When Suzanne was aggressive at home, her mother either instructed her to go to her room or removed something that Suzanne considered positive (e.g., a treat).

Below is an excerpt from the CPII, which illustrates Suzanne's mother providing a description of her concerns about Suzanne's behavior at home.

Consultant: Okay, so we talked about her not following rules; we talked about her being aggressive — meaning hitting and kicking — we talked about ripping up things that don't belong to her, about her being clingy, and about her arguing with her sisters. Now, if you were going to pick something that is the most destructive for her and most disturbing to you, what do you think is the most important thing to be working on?

Parent: I think the, um, destructiveness and aggressiveness.

Consultant: Okay, so now give me as many examples as you can of what she does when she is destructive and aggressive.

Parent: Um, tearing up the things that don't belong to her.

Consultant: Okay.

Parent: And she gets either Crayola or a marker and writes on the walls.

Consultant: Uh huh.

Parent: And she has this big wheel and she, like on purpose, she runs us over and she would run over our feet.

Consultant: Uh huh.

Parent: And she hits and kicks her sisters.

Consultant: Okay.

Parent: She never hit my brother, but I don't think she's gonna either.

Consultant: She might not want to try that one, huh? You said something about hitting herself and hitting her sisters.

Parent: Yeah.

Consultant: More examples?

Parent: Just what I said before.

Consultant: Okay. Let me sum up what we have here, aggressiveness is your main concern including the things you mentioned such as destroying things, hitting and kicking.

Parent: Yeah.

Aggressive behavior was not identified by Suzanne's teacher as a concern at school. Her teacher noted that at times Suzanne had difficulty paying attention to the speaker during structured times. For example, during circle time when the teacher addressed the group, Suzanne often played with toys or distracted others around her. Therefore, it was determined that the focus for consultation in school would be to increase Suzanne's attentive behavior during large-group activities. Suzanne had the most difficulty during structured times (i.e., large-group, small-group) and also had difficulty if she was seated next to another inattentive child. When Suzanne was inattentive, her teacher redirected her, which appeared to be an effective strategy with Suzanne.

To get a better idea of how often Suzanne was aggressive toward people or objects, her mother was asked to estimate how often these behaviors occurred. She estimated that at home Suzanne's aggressive behavior occurred approximately 5 times a day, with a duration of 5-10 minutes. When asked to rate severity on a scale of 0 to 10 (0 being not severe and 10 being very severe), she rated Suzanne's aggressive behavior as a 9. At school, Suzanne's teacher estimated that Suzanne's inattentive behavior occurred approximately 1 or 2 times a day and lasted 2 or 3 minutes. She rated Suzanne's inattentive behavior as a 2 on a scale from 0 to 10. The tentative goal decided upon for home was reducing the incidents of aggressive acts to 2 times a day. At school, the tentative goal was to eliminate Suzanne's inattentive behavior during large group time.

Problem Analysis

The goal of the problem-analysis session was to review baseline data and discuss the intervention plan. The Conjoint Problem Analysis Interview (CPAI) was approximately an hour. Suzanne's mother and teacher collected data for 2 weeks. Data collection consisted of using an event recording method. Suzanne's mother recorded the number of times per day that Suzanne was aggressive toward people or objects; her teacher recorded Suzanne's inattentive behavior during structured times. The baseline data that her mother collected revealed that Suzanne was aggressive at home an average of 6 times per day, with a range of 2-9 times per day. Suzanne's teacher indicated that at school Suzanne was not paying attention to the speaker during structured times an average of 3 times per day, with a range of 2-4 times per day. Suzanne's mother's and teacher's accounts of antecedents and consequences provided additional information. In general, her mother stated that at home, Suzanne often was aggressive when given a directive or when she was not getting her way.

Below is an excerpt from the CPAI, which illustrates Suzanne's mother providing a description of the antecedents to Suzanne's aggressive behavior.

Consultant: Did you notice anything that was happening before the aggressive outbursts? Did you notice anything going on, like you said
it seems to be in relation to when you gave her a directive, did
it seem to be...

Parent: Not necessarily.

Consultant: Okay.

Parent: This is one of the best places, when she would, you know, if I
gave her directions, but not necessarily, because sometimes she
just lashes out and do something to one of her sisters.

Consultant: Did you notice anything going on before, maybe you saw a
pattern or something, we are trying to look for some pattern of
what is setting her off. Sometimes it seems like it is just out of
the blue, that she is just doing it...

Parent: Yeah, sometimes it is out of the blue and sometimes when I give
her the directions...

Consultant: Okay.

Parent: ...and then other times it's like her sisters have something she
wants

Consultant: Mm hmm.

Parent: You know she will do it then...

Consultant: Okay, those are good examples.

At school, Suzanne's teacher identified structured activities as times
when she had difficulty paying attention. The consequences following
Suzanne's aggressive behavior at home were either sending her to her room
or taking a treat away from her. At school, Suzanne's teacher redirected her
when she was inattentive or distracting others.

Treatment (Plan) Implementation

The intervention consisted of implementing a manual-based treatment
program developed for preschool children exhibiting externalizing behavior
problems. The treatment manual was developed specifically for the Head
Start population and included both a teacher and a parent manual version. The
first step of the intervention consisted of *skill selection* and *goal-setting*. The
goal for school, selected by the teacher and consultant, was paying attention
to the speaker during large-group activity. The goal selected for home by the
parent and consultant involved following adult directions. Daily and weekly
goals were set up for both home and school. When Suzanne met her daily
goal, she received a sticker. At the end of the week, if Suzanne met her weekly

goal at home, her mother sent a positive note to her teacher at school, and when she met her weekly goal at school, a positive note was sent home. The part of the manual that was implemented involved the teacher and parent setting up activities in the classroom or home between Suzanne and one peer to help Suzanne practice and develop her social skills.

The next section of the manual was called *differential attention* and involved the parent and teacher attending to Suzanne while she was playing, rewarding her for appropriate behavior, and ignoring her inappropriate behavior. The teacher and parent also used *instruction-giving* skills to get Suzanne to do the things that she is asked to do and to stop doing things they find undesirable. The last section of the manual to be implemented was the parent using *time away* to decrease the frequency of Suzanne's undesirable behavior. Time away was the last section of the manual to be implemented. However, Suzanne's mother indicated that because instruction-giving was successful at getting Suzanne to follow directions and refrain from undesirable behaviors, time away was not necessary.

Treatment (Plan) Evaluation

A Conjoint Treatment Evaluation Interview (CTEI) was conducted upon completion of the intervention. The intervention was evaluated through direct observations at school by observers and also by teacher- and parent- completed goal attainment scales. The observer conducted 18 20-minute observations (6 during baseline, 9 during treatment, and 3 at follow-up). The data collection procedure used by the observers consisted of a 30-second partial interval recording of how often Suzanne followed teacher directions (Target Behavior 1 [TB 1]) and controlled her temper in conflict situations (Target Behavior 2 [TB 2]).[1] In addition, the observers collected data on a comparison peer who was targeted by the teacher as having average skills. Interrater agreement also was obtained during every 3rd observation and resulted in an average of 89% agreement between two observers.

---

[1] Since Suzanne's inattentive behavior was not viewed by her teacher as a significant problem, it was decided that the independent observers would monitor her home target behaviors in the school environment because they caused the greatest concern. The target behaviors of following directions and controlling temper in conflict situations were thus selected for observation by independent observers at school. However, Suzanne's teacher continued to use an event-recording method to count the number of times per day that Suzanne was inattentive during large-group time at school. In addition, Suzanne's mother used an event-recording method to record the number of times per day that Suzanne was aggressive at home.

The results of the intervention are summarized in Figure 6.5. Data collected by the observers revealed that Suzanne's ability to follow teacher directions was variable. However, during treatment and follow-up, her behaviors showed a slight increase and were more consistent. Suzanne followed teacher directions 100% of the time during treatment and follow-up with the exception of 2 days during treatment. On those days, she followed teacher directions 50% and 0% of the time. Her comparison peer followed directions 100% of the time during treatment observations. In addition, Suzanne was able to control her temper in conflict situations 100% of the time, with the exception of 1 day during treatment when she was confronted with 4 conflict situations, and controlled her temper in 3 of the 4 situations. Suzanne's ability to control her temper in conflict situations was similar to that of the comparison peer.

Goal attainment scales also were used to monitor Suzanne's behavior both at home and in school. Goal attainment scaling provides a method for quantifying parents' and teachers' reports of treatment progress with regard to a target behavior and problem situation. The basic elements of a goal attainment scale are a 5-point scale ranging from +2 to −2 and descriptions of the target behavior and problem situation that correspond to the following conditions: best possible behavior (+2), no change in behavior (0), and worst possible behavior (−2). The target behavior selected for the goal attainment scale at school was paying attention during large-group activity. At home, there were both a short-term and a long-term goal. The short-term goal was following adult directions; the long-term goal was decreasing aggressive behavior. At school Suzanne met her goal (+2) by the 9th week of treatment and continued to receive weekly ratings of +2 throughout the remainder of the treatment. At home, Suzanne met both the long- and short-term goals by the 6th week of treatment and continued to receive ratings of +2 throughout the remainder of the treatment.

Following the intervention, Suzanne's mother and teacher completed the SSRS and CBCL-TRF a second time. At this administration, Suzanne obtained SSRS Total scores of 106 and 101 on the parent and teacher forms, respectively. These scores revealed substantial improvements in social skills across both settings. Problem Behavior scores also improved. Responses on the CBCL indicated improvements across the Total scale, and the Internalizing and Externalizing factors, with the greatest improvements noted in the area of Externalizing behaviors (a decrease of 1.5 SD from pre- to posttest). Teacher responses on the TRF continued to be within the average range.

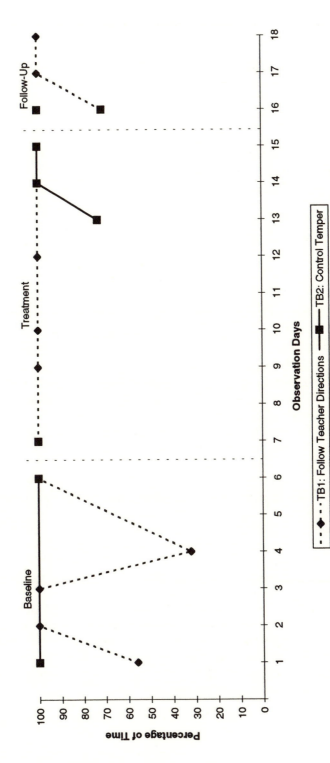

Figure 6.5. Direct observation data collected on two target behaviors (following directions and controlling temper) by an independent observer.

Below is an excerpt from the CTEI that illustrates a description of Suzanne's mother's and teacher's feedback regarding the effectiveness of the treatment.

Consultant: If you remember when we met the first time, you wanted to reduce the aggressive acts at home to two per day. Has that goal been met?

Parent: Yeah, it's been met.

Consultant: And what would you guess, how often is she aggressive?

Parent: It's probably once a day or even, not even in the day...

Consultant: Mm hmm.

Parent: So, it depends on the situation.

Consultant: Mm hmm, so let's say in a week, how many times a week do you think?

Parent: Two to three.

Consultant: Okay, and how about at school, you wanted zero inattentive times. Has that goal been met?

Teacher: Um, yes, some days that definitely happens.

Consultant: Some days, so how many times a week would you say...

Teacher: That she was inattentive? I would probably say two to three.

Consultant: Okay, do you think that the behavior program that we used was responsible for the change in Suzanne's behavior?

Parent: Yep, definitely.

Consultant: Was there any part of the program that you thought was especially effective with her?

Parent: Um, let's see, let me think, especially, I think the warning, you know, um...

Consultant: During the instruction-giving, when you gave a warning?

Parent: Yeah, right, you know if she didn't comply.

Consultant: Okay, how about at school, do you think that the behavior program was responsible for the change in...

Teacher: Yes.

Consultant: ...Suzanne's behavior? Were there any parts that you thought were particularly helpful or effective?

Teacher: Um, specifically when I would, um, approach Suzanne when she came into the classroom and speak to her about "Do you remember what we talked about and how we need to sit attentively at large circle and be listening?"

Consultant: The goal setting?

Teacher: Yeah, the goal setting.

Treatment Integrity

Treatment integrity data also were collected throughout treatment. Both Suzanne's mother and her teacher were asked to report each of the steps in the specific section of the manual that they were able to implement during a particular week. The results of the treatment integrity assessment are summarized as follows: Overall, treatment integrity data were adequate, with an average of 84% of the steps being implemented at home and 93% at school over the course of treatment.

Case Discussion

In general, Suzanne's mother and teacher reported that Suzanne responded well to the intervention. Her mother reported that instruction-giving was a particularly useful part of the treatment manual (especially the "if-then" approach). Suzanne's teacher reported that goal-setting was effective with Suzanne. Both her mother and her teacher stated that the program was responsible for the change in Suzanne's behavior. In addition, her teacher reported that many of the strategies were useful and she intended to try them with other children in her classroom. Suzanne's mother indicated that she learned many new skills and that she would continue to use these strategies with Suzanne as well as her other two children. Suzanne's mother and teacher both reported that the goal of increasing Suzanne's overall appropriate behavior was effectively met.

AGGRESSIVE AND TERRITORIAL BEHAVIORS: THE CASE OF KEN

Ingrid Sladeczek

Background Information

The child in this case was a 3-year, 11-month-old boy named "Ken," referred by his mother for conduct problems. More specifically, Ken's mother indicated that he had difficulties with cooperation, assertion, and self-control. Further, he exhibited severe temper tantrums in the home. Ken's teacher also viewed him as experiencing social skill deficits, but saw his problems as being less severe than did his mother. Temper tantrums were not observed at school, although Ken tended to "screech" when other children invaded his "space."

Conjoint consultation was initiated at the beginning of the school year. The Conjoint Problem Identification Interview (CPII), Conjoint Problem Analysis Interview (CPAI), and Conjoint Treatment Evaluation Interview (CTEI) were conducted at Ken's preschool.

Problem Identification

The first stage of CBC, problem identification, was implemented to specify the problem or problems to be targeted. Specifically, the CPII was conducted to (1) review general characteristics that might be related to Ken's social skill deficits and problem behaviors, (2) identify the specific concerns of Ken's mother and teacher, (3) generate a consultation/intervention goal, and (4) develop data collection procedures for the baseline phase of the program. As part of the problem-identification process, both Ken's mother and teacher completed the Social Skills Rating System (Parent or Teacher Form) (SSRS-P, SSRS-T) (Gresham & Elliott, 1990). His teacher also completed the Teacher Report Form (TRF) (Achenbach, 1991b). Both Ken's mother and teacher participated in the CPII.

The SSRS (parent and teacher versions) measures a child's social skills and examines problem behaviors compared to other children of the same age from a national sample. Standard scores (mean = 100; SD = 15) are derived from item responses. Ken scored a standard score of 70 on the Social Skills scale (high scores reflect desirable behaviors) and a standard score of 143 on the Problem Behaviors scale (high scores reflect problem behaviors). Thus, Ken's mother viewed him as having fewer skills related to cooperation, assertion, self-control, and responsibility compared to other children his age. The mother did not complete the CBCL. Ken's teacher did not see significant social skills deficits or problem behaviors in the classroom. However, on the TRF, she indicated that he evidenced some externalizing problems (e.g., fidgeting or moving excessively) (T-score = 55), but experienced substantially more internalizing problems (T-score = 65) (e.g., acts sad or depressed, self-conscious or easily embarrassed, complains of loneliness) compared to other children his age. T- scores have a mean of 50 and a standard deviation of 10; scores between 40 and 60 are considered "average."

The consultant met with Ken's mother and teacher for approximately 1 hour for the CPII. During the CPII, it was determined that the focus for consultation in the home would be to increase Ken's appropriate social behaviors and decrease his problem behaviors. Specifically, Ken's territorial behavior and temper tantrums were of extreme concern. Ken often screamed when he perceived his mother to be disturbing his space. Further, Ken's frequent temper tantrums both at home and in public settings were extremely disturbing to his mother. Temper tantrum behaviors included screaming, hitting, and kicking either the person with him or nearby objects. His mother also reported that Ken was often aggressive when he was asked to follow a directive. When Ken was aggressive at home or in public, she either physically removed him (while he was kicking and screaming) or tried to implement a time-away procedure. Occasionally, she raised her voice and shook him to stop his tantrum. Below is an excerpt from the CPII:

Parent: I bought Ken a bike with training wheels, and when we were trying it out, I mentioned to him before we left that we would switch from one thing to the next, that mommy has to go inside and work.

Teacher: Mm hmm.

Parent: I'll tell Ken before we go out that this is going to happen. You know, I'll explain to him that when it's time to go, mommy will tell you it's time to go and we have to switch to do something else. Maybe you will have to help me do laundry or something. And when it's time to switch, then, it's like he doesn't remember what I told him, and I have to carry, literally carry him while he's kicking and carry the bike in as well and it's very, very hard on me.

Teacher: I don't see him having a lot of trouble transitioning here because I use a lot of foreshadowing as well. For example, that we are going do this, but in so many minutes or whatever when we say or when we hear a sound (e.g., bell), then it's time to put the toys away, that kind of thing. I think that he is getting the reactions from you that he wants, you know. You could just let him scream and carry the bike in. I mean, he is not going to want to see you and his bike go in the building and not follow you.

Parent: But I did, I do that, and he does follow me but he screams. I don't want the whole community disrupted just because Ken is unhappy.

Aggressive or tantrumming behaviors were not identified as a concern at school. However, Ken's teacher expressed concern regarding his territorial behavior with peers and his screeching when children intruded upon his area. Although Ken's teacher stressed that it was appropriate to feel anger, she tried to teach the children to express their anger with words. His teacher also reported that Ken often liked to play alone. He played with other children, but seldom initiated play behavior. To obtain an accurate account of the severity of Ken's aggressive/territorial behaviors, his mother and teacher were asked to keep a daily log of how often these behaviors occurred and bring this information to the CPAI.

Problem Analysis

The second stage of the conjoint consultation process, problem analysis, was initiated with the CPAI. The purpose of the CPAI was twofold. First, the data collected by both the mother and the teacher were examined to obtain an indication of the severity of Ken's problem behaviors. Second, a treatment program was discussed, agreed upon, and then implemented.

During baseline, Ken's mother recorded any incident of Ken's aggressive and territorial behaviors. The frequency of these behaviors ranged from 0 to as many as 7 incidents per day (see Figure 6.6). The baseline data that the teacher collected indicated a frequency of aggressive/territorial behaviors from a low of 1 per day to as many as 5 incidents per day.

Below is an excerpt from the CPAI.

Consultant: What happened on the 27th of the month?

Parent: There was lots of trouble with Ken. He wants to lunge at people, lunge from time to time. I've noticed this throughout the week. I'm sure there's some that I skipped. He puts up his fist as if he wants to punch somebody in the face, and he just lunges. And he did a lot of that lunging on the 27th. I wrote down that he was a lot of trouble.

Consultant: How many times did he lunge at someone?

Parent: I would say a good estimate would be five.

Consultant: OK.

Parent: He just wouldn't take any counsel, he would not listen to reason.

Consultant: OK.

Parent: I tell him to go to his room to chill out, or anything.

Consultant: What happened on the 28th of the month?

Parent: I've been telling Ken that it is okay to be angry. It's okay to cry. It's okay, but we just have to do it in moderation, you know, you can be angry but then count to five. One, two, three, four, five. And I've been trying to teach Ken to use anger control, using those words. We need to have anger control, so let's try. When you feel a little bit of pressure, count to five. Maybe step in your room or something like that and just wait it out and then come back fresh. So that's the approach I tried.

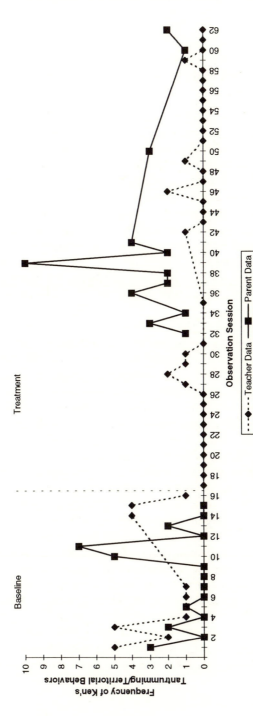

Figure 6.6. Frequency of Ken's aggressive/territorial behaviors as observed by his mother and teacher.

Consultant: Has Ken used this approach?
   Parent: He used it on me. He said to me, count five mom, you look like you're angry. [Laughs] I think it's in his mind. He just has to apply it.

Discussion of antecedent and consequent conditions surrounding Ken's problem behaviors provided additional information. Antecedent conditions for Ken's aggressive/tantrumming behavior often included simply a request by his mother to do a particular task. He often pushed his mother, at which point she would talk to him and indicate that his behavior was inappropriate. Subsequently, she would institute a time-away procedure. The teacher reported that Ken mainly responded in an aggressive manner when he did not want other children joining an activity in which he was engaged. When Ken yelled and screamed at other children, or became physically aggressive, he was given a warning and/or immediately placed in time-away (depending on the severity of the behavior he exhibited). Again, it is important to remember that in general, Ken's teacher did not see a significant problem with his behavior at school.

The intervention consisted of implementing a manual-based treatment program developed for preschool children exhibiting externalizing behavior problems. The treatment manual was developed specifically for a preschool population and included parent and teacher versions. Because the major goal of treatment was to decrease Ken's aggressive/tantrumming behaviors, it was agreed upon by both his mother and teacher that for the first 4 weeks, implementation of appropriate behavior management techniques would be the focus of intervention efforts. Specifically, skills included *attending to* Ken and *rewarding* him when he behaved appropriately, and *ignoring* him when he behaved inappropriately. Of course, it was not always possible to ignore all of Ken's aggressive/tantrumming behaviors, so his mother and teacher had to make important decisions when using the differential attending skills. *Instruction-giving* skills were the focus of the second 8 weeks of treatment. Differential attention skills were not abandoned, but instruction-giving skills were added to them. Instruction-giving skills were used to get Ken to do things that the mother or teacher requested him to do. These skills were also used to get Ken to stop performing undesirable behaviors. Some of the characteristics that increased the effectiveness of instruction-giving included (1) being specific and direct, (2) giving one command at a time, (3) following a command with a wait of 8–10 seconds, (4) praising Ken when he followed directions, and (5) issuing a warning and a consequence if Ken did not follow directions. The last 4 weeks were spent correctly implementing a time-away procedure (as a last resort) if Ken continued to act aggressively or for serious violations of classroom rules. *Time-away* involved removing Ken from a conflicting situation where events were encouraging his aggressive behaviors.

Treatment Evaluation

The intervention was evaluated on a continual basis through several mechanisms: (1) teacher and parent observations of Ken's aggressive/territorial behaviors, (2) independent observations of Ken's and a comparison child's aggressive/territorial behaviors at school, (3) goal attainment ratings by the mother and teacher on a weekly basis, and (4) measurement of treatment integrity.

Data collected across conditions by Ken's mother and teacher are depicted in Figure 6.6. Observations by Ken's mother and teacher over the course of treatment suggested that in general, Ken's aggressive/territorial behaviors decreased from baseline to treatment. However, there were some fluctuations during treatment, most notably on Observation Day 39 (Treatment Day 23), when he exhibited 10 undesirable behaviors at home.

An independent observer conducted 17 20-minute observations (6 during baseline and 11 during treatment). Follow-up observations occurred at a later date. The observer saw very few aggressive/territorial behaviors at school. In fact, Ken spent no more than 10% of his time engaging in such behaviors; a comparison child exhibited even fewer target behaviors.

Goal attainment scales were also used to monitor Ken's behavior at home and at school. Goal attainment scaling provides a mechanism for quantifying mothers' and teachers' reports of treatment progress with regard to the target behavior and problem situations. The basic component of this procedure was a 5-point scale ranging from a +2 to a −2 that corresponded with descriptions of the target behavior. A score of +2 can be viewed as the best possible behavior being exhibited; a −2 indicates the worst possible behavior, and a 0 indicates little or no change in behavior. For example, a +2 indicated that "Ken acts appropriately, verbalizes frustrations with words, allows classmates to engage in activities with him. He almost always (90% of the time) responds appropriately when someone enters his space." A −2 indicated that "Ken frequently exhibits acting-out behaviors when other classmates or adults approach his space. Ken acts appropriately less than 20% of the time." Similar descriptions were provided for Ken's mother.

Ken's teacher consistently rated the attainment of goals higher than did his mother. This rating is not surprising, since Ken's behavior was more severe at home. Specifically, across 16 days on which ratings were made, his teacher reported a mean goal attainment score of +1 (range = −2 to +2). Across 14 days, his mother reported a mean goal attainment score of 0 (range = −1 to +1).

During the CTEI, the efficacy of the treatment procedures was ascertained. An excerpt from the CTEI follows:

Consultant: How has Ken been doing, overall?

Teacher: I think that he understands now that he has control over himself, that there are some places that he needs to have more control and he's able to do that. We went to the library on Friday, and I remember, you [to parent] had told me at the beginning of the year that he's so paranoid about the library, because you cue him every time you go in there, that it is a quiet place and you know how to behave and yet when you get in there you are real nervous or you used to be real nervous because you are afraid he's going to start to yell or do what he's not supposed to.

Parent: I don't have time to take him a lot, but the babysitter does quite a bit, once a week at least, for reading. She told me that he was real disruptive.

Teacher: He was also very good. I guess we went on Friday to pick out a movie and I had twenty kids there. He was very good. He knew exactly what to do. He whispered and said, "I see that there's a Big Bird movie over there, maybe we could see that one too." We pulled out the Big Bird movie and the kids voted on which one they wanted. He said it in a whispering voice.

Parent: Good.

Teacher: You know, I was real impressed that he was one of the more quiet kids, but what we talked about on the way to the library was, "Look, all you kids remember that this is a library. It's a quiet place, people are in there reading. It's not a loud place." So foreshadowing, foreshadowing works great with him, just at the meeting, the parent meeting, he was so very good and all the parents complimented him, you know.

Parent: I noticed that.

Teacher: So, foreshadowing works, definitely.

Ken's mother indicated that she had seen "...remarkable positive changes," but stated that the time-away procedures had not been effective in decreasing or alleviating his aggressive behaviors at home. Ken's teacher reported that she had seen a significant amount of improvement in his mother's ability to deal with Ken's challenging behaviors and also an improvement in Ken's ability to control his negative behaviors. Further, he appeared to be more comfortable in allowing other children to become involved in his activities. Approximately 1 month after treatment, his mother indicated that she had started a very successful charting program of Ken's behaviors, wherein she was rewarding him with stickers for appropriate behaviors. Also, the home situation had improved dramatically. Both Ken's mother and his teacher reported that many of the strategies were useful. Posttest measures suggested an improvement in Ken's social skills and a reduction in his problem behaviors. However, responses on the CBCL and TRF continued to indicate a concern with internalizing behaviors (e.g., is sometimes shy or timid) and externalizing behaviors.

Treatment Integrity

Treatment integrity data were also collected throughout treatment. Both Ken's mother and his teacher were asked how many skills they had been able to complete during the different phases of implementation. Completion of skills varied between 60% and 80% for the mother. In particular, ignoring and time-away procedures were more difficult for Ken's mother to implement. Completion of skills ranged from 80% to 100% for Ken's teacher.

Case Discussion

This case demonstrated the utility of CBC with a preschool child exhibiting aggressive and tantrumming behaviors. A decrease in Ken's problem behaviors was noted at home and school during treatment implementation, although his performance was somewhat variable. It was recommended to Ken's mother and teacher that future intervention strategies focus on positive feedback (e.g., praise, attention, positive reinforcers) to reinforce appropriate behaviors. It was noted that Ken should be encouraged to initiate conversations and play with peers and be reinforced for allowing other adults and children to join him in activities.

Ken reportedly responded well to a charting system wherein his behaviors were recorded and he was rewarded with stickers and positive attention when he behaved appropriately. Concrete expression of expectations and implementation of a reward system for desirable behaviors were recommended. In addition, it was noted that consequences for inappropriate behavior should be made clear and carried out consistently.

Since Ken was still exhibiting internalizing behavior problems (e.g., feeling lonely) following the consultation treatment, it was recommended that situations be set up that facilitate his interactions with other children. Small-group activities both at home and at school were examples of strategies that encourage such interactive behavior.

It was also recommended that Ken be taught how to release his anger in more appropriate, nonaggressive ways. For example, his mother was told to have him identify his feelings, ask him why he feels that way, and discuss alternative means to handle problem situations without aggressive behaviors.

DISCUSSION QUESTIONS

1 | What are some specific target behaviors that might be targeted in conjoint behavioral consultation case studies?

2 | What are some examples from the various case studies that highlight important benefits of CBC over consultation with a teacher or a parent only?

3 | How can various measures be combined to assess CBC outcomes? In other words, what outcomes are important to assess and how can their results be integrated and interpreted?

4 | What are some strengths and weaknesses of each of the case studies?

References

Abidin, R. R. (1983). *Parenting Stress Inventory*. Charlottesville, NC: Pediatric Psychology Press.

Achenbach, T. M. (1991a). *Manual for the Child Behavior Checklist/4–18 and 1991 Profile*. Burlington, VT: University of Vermont, Department of Psychiatry.

Achenbach, T. M. (1991b). *Manual for the Teacher's Report Form and 1991 Profile*. Burlington, VT: University of Vermont, Department of Psychiatry.

Alpert, J. L., & Yammer, M. D. (1983). Research in school consultation: A content analysis of selected journals. *Professional Psychology: Research and Practice, 14*, 604–612.

Anderson, C. (1983). An ecological developmental model for a family orientation in school psychology. *Journal of School Psychology, 21*, 179–189.

Anderson, T. K., Kratochwill, T. R., & Bergan, J. R. (1986). Training teachers in behavioral consultation and therapy: An analysis of verbal behaviors. *Journal of School Psychology, 24*, 229–241.

Apter, S. J. (1982). *Troubled children/Troubled systems*. Elmsford, NY: Pergamon Press.

Apter, S. J., & Conoley, J. C. (1984). *Childhood behavior disorder and emotional disturbance*. Englewood Cliffs, NJ: Prentice-Hall.

Barclay, J. R. (1978). *Appraising individual differences in the elementary classroom: A manual for the Barclay Classroom Climate Inventory*. Lexington, KY: Educational Skills Development Inc.

Barkley, R. A. (1990). *Attention deficit hyperactivity disorder: A handbook for diagnosis and treatment*. New York: Guilford.

Barkley, R. A. (1987). *Defiant children: A clinician's manual for parent training*. New York: Guilford Press.

Becher, R. M. (1986). Parent involvement: A review of research and principles of successful practice. In L. G. Katz (Ed.), *Current topics in early childhood education* (Vol. VI) (pp. 85–122). Norwood, NJ: Ablex Publishing Corporation.

Beck, A. T., Ward, C. H., Mendelson, M., Mock, J., & Erbaugh, J. (1961). An inventory for measuring depression. *Archives of General Psychiatry, 4*, 561–571.

Becker, H. J., & Epstein, J. L. (1982). Parent involvement: A survey of teacher practices. *The Elementary School Journal, 83*, 85–102.

Bergan, J. R., Byrnes, I., & Kratochwill, T. R. (1979). Effects of behavioral and medical models of consultation on teacher expectancies and instruction of a hypothetical child. *Journal of School Psychology, 17*, 307–316.

Bergan, J. R., & Duley, S. (1981). Behavioral consultation with families. In R. W. Henderson (Ed.), *Parent–child interactions: Theory, research, and prospects* (pp. 265–291). New York: Academic Press.

Bergan, J. R., & Kratochwill, T. R. (1990). *Behavioral consultation and therapy*. New York: Plenum Press.

Bergan, J. R., & Neumann, A. (1980). The identification of resources and constraints influencing plan design in consultation. *Journal of School Psychology, 18*, 317–323.

Bergan, J. R., Reddy, L. A., Feld, J. K., Sladeczek, I. E., & Schwarz, R. D. (1991, August). Parent consultation, school socioeconomic status, and summer learning. Paper presented at the 98th Annual Meeting of the American Psychological Association, San Francisco.

Bergan, J. R., & Tombari, M. L. (1975). The analysis of verbal interactions occurring during consultation. *Journal of School Psychology, 13*, 209–226.

Bergan, J. R., & Tombari, M. L. (1976). Consultant skill and efficiency and the implementation and outcomes of consultation. *Journal of School Psychology, 14*, 3–14.

Bijou, S. W. (1984). Parent training: Where it came from and where it's at. In R. F. Dangel & R. A. Polster (Eds.), *Parent training* (pp. 15–26). New York: Guilford Press.

Bijou, S. W., Peterson, R. F., & Ault, M. H. (1968). A method to integrate descriptive and experimental field studies at the level of data and empirical concepts. *Journal of Applied Behavior Analysis, 1*, 175–191.

Bijou, S. W., Peterson, R. F., Harris, F. R., Allen, K. E., & Johnson, M. S. (1969). Methodology for experimental studies of young children in natural settings. *Psychological Record, 19*, 177–210.

Braun, L., & Swap, S. (1987). *Building home–school partnerships with America's changing families*. Boston: Wheelock College.

Bronfenbrenner, U. (1977). Toward an experimental ecology of human development. *American Psychologist, 32*, 513–529.

Brown, D., Pryzwansky, W. B., & Schulte, A. C. (1995). *Psychological consultation: Introduction to theory and practice* (3rd ed.). Boston: Allyn & Bacon.

Carlson, C. I. (1987). Resolving school problems with structural family therapy. *School Psychology Review, 16*, 457–468.

Carlson, C. I., Hickman, J., & Horton, C. B. (1992). From blame to solutions: Solution-oriented family–school consultation. In S. L. Christenson & J. C. Conoley (Eds.), *Home–school collaboration: Enhancing children's academic and social competence* (pp. 193–213). Silver Spring, MD: National Association of School Psychologists.

Carr, E. G. (1994). Emerging themes in the functional analysis of problem behavior. *Journal of Applied Behavior Analysis, 27*, 393–399.

Carrington Rotto, P., & Kratochwill, T. R. (1994). Behavioral consultation with parents: Using competency-based training to modify child noncompliance. *School Psychology Review, 23*, 669–693.

Cataldo, M. F. (1984). Clinical considerations in training parents of children with special problems. In R. E. Dangel & R. A. Polster (Eds.), *Parent training* (pp. 329–357). New York: Guilford Press.

Chavkin, N. F., & Williams, D. L. (1985). *Parent involvement in education project. Executive summary of the final report.* Austin, TX: Southwest Educational Developmental Laboratory, Document Reproduction Service. (ERIC No. ED 266 874).

Children's Defense Fund (1989). *A vision for America's future.* Washington DC: Author.

Christenson, S. L., Abery, B., & Weinberg, R. A. (1986). An alternative model for the delivery of psychological services in the school in the community. In S. N. Elliott & J. C. Witt (Eds.), *The delivery of psychological services in the schools: Concepts, processes, and issues* (pp. 349–392). Hillsdale, NJ: Lawrence Erlbaum.

Christenson, S. L., & Cleary, M. (1990). Consultation and the parent–educator partnership: A perspective. *Journal of Educational and Psychological Consultation, 1,* 219–241.

Christenson, S. L., & Conoley, J. C. (1992) (Eds.). *Home–school collaboration: Building a fundamental educational resource.* Silver Spring, MD: National Association of School Psychologists.

Christenson, S. L., Rounds, T., & Gorney, D. (1992). Family factors and student achievement: An avenue to increase students' success. *School Psychology Quarterly, 7,* 178–206.

Cialdini, R. B. (1993). *Influence: Science and practice* (3rd ed.). New York: HarperCollins.

Cobb, D. E., & Medway, F. J. (1978). Determinants of effectiveness in parent consultation. *Journal of Community Psychology, 6,* 229–240.

Colton, D., Sheridan, S. M., Jenson, W. R., & Malm, K. (1995, March). Behavioral consultation with parents and teachers: Promoting cooperative peer interactions with boys with ADHD. Paper presented at the annual meeting of the National Association of School Psychologists, Chicago, IL.

Comer, J. P. (1984). Home–school relationships as they affect the academic success of children. *Education and Urban Society, 16,* 323–337.

Comer, J. P., & Haynes, N. M. (1991). Parent involvement in schools: An ecological approach. *The Elementary School Journal, 91,* 271–277.

Conners, K. C. (1990). *Conners' Rating Scales Manual.* North Tonawanda, NY: Multi-Health Systems, Inc.

Conoley, J. C. (1987a). Strategic family intervention: Three cases of school-aged children. *School Psychology Review, 16,* 469–486.

Conoley, J. C. (1987b). Schools and families: Theoretical and practical bridges. *Professional School Psychology, 2,* 191–203.

Conoley, J. C., & Sheridan, S. M. (in press). Pediatric traumatic brain injury: Challenges and interventions for families. *Journal of Learning Disabilities.*

Cooper, J. O., Heron, T. E., & Heward, W. I. (1987). *Applied behavior analysis.* Columbus, OH: Merrill Publishing Co.

Cooper, L. J., Wacker, D. P., Sasso, G. M., Reimers, T. M., & Donn, L. K. (1990). Using parents as therapists to evaluate appropriate behavior of their children: Application to a tertiary diagnostic clinic. *Journal of Applied Behavior Analysis, 23,* 285–296.

Dadds, M. R., & Powell, M. (in press). An examination of sampling and sex effects in the relationship of marital discord to childhood aggression, anxiety, and immaturity. *Journal of Clinical Child Psychology.*

Dangel, R. F., & Polster, R. A. (1984). *Parent training: Foundations of research and practice.* New York: Guilford Press.

Dangel, R. F., & Polster, R. A. (1988). *Teaching child management skills*. Elmsford, NY: Pergamon Press.

Dauber, S. L., & Epstein, J. L. (1989). *Parent attitudes and practices of parent involvement in inner-city elementary and middle schools*. Baltimore, MD: Center for Research on Elementary and Middle Schools.

Davis, W. E. (1991, August). Promoting effective communication between schools and parents of disadvantaged students. Paper presented at the 99th Annual Convention of the American Psychological Association, San Francisco, CA.

Davis, W. E., & McCaul, E. J. (1991). *The emerging crisis: Current and projected status of children in the United States*. Orono, ME: College of Education, University of Maine.

Dembo, M. H., Sweitzer, M., & Lauritzen, P. (1985). An evaluation of group parent education: Behavioral, PET, and Adlerian programs. *Review of Educational Research, 55*, 155–200.

Derogatis, L. R., & Melisaratos, N. (1983). The Brief Symptom Inventory: A preliminary report. *Psychological Medicine, 13*, 595–605.

Dinkmeyer, D., & McKay, G. (1976). *Systematic training for effective parenting*. Circle Pines, MN: American Guidance Services.

Dombalis, A. O., & Erchul, W. P. (1987). Multiple family group therapy: A review of its applicability to the pracatice of school psychology. *School Psychology Review, 16*, 487–497.

Drabman, R. S., Hammer, D., & Rosenbaum, M. S. (1979). Assessing generalization in behavior modification with children: The generalization map. *Behavioral Assessment, 1*, 203–219.

Dumas, J. E. (1989). Treating antisocial behavior in children: Child and family approaches. *Clinical Psychology Review, 9*, 197–222.

Dunst, C. J., & Trivette, C. M. (1987). Enabling and empowering families: Conceptual and intervention issues. *School Psychology Review, 16*, 443–456.

DuPaul, G., & Eckert, T. (1994). The effects of social skills curricula: Now you see them, now you don't. *School Psychology Quarterly, 9*, 113–132.

Durand, L. M., & Crimmins, D. B. (1988). The Motivation Assessment Scale: An administrative manual. Unpublished manuscript. Albany, NY: State University of New York at Albany.

Educational Testing Service (1992). *America's smallest school: The family*. Princeton, NJ: Author.

Elliott, S. N., & Von Brock Treuting, M. (1991). The Behavior Intervention Rating Scale: Development and validation of a pretreatment acceptability and effectiveness measure. *Journal of School Psychology, 29*, 43–51.

Epstein, J. L. (1982, March). *Student reactions to teachers' practices of parent involvement*. Paper presented at the annual meeting of the American Educational Research Association, New York.

Epstein, J. L. (1984, Winter). School policy and parent involvement: Research results. *Educational Horizons*, pp. 70–72.

Epstein, J. L. (1986). Parents' reactions to teacher practices of parent involvement. *The Elementary School Journal, 86*, 277–294.

Epstein, J. L. (1987, January). What principals should know about parent involvement. *Principal*, pp. 6–9.

Epstein, J. L. (1990). Single parents and the school: Effects of marital status on parent and teacher interactions. In M. T. Hallinan, D. M. Klein, & J. Glass (Eds.), *Change in societal institutions* (pp. 91–121). New York: Plenum Press.

Epstein, J. L. (in press). The effects of teacher practices of parent involvement. In S. Silvern (Ed.), *Advances in reading language research, Vol. 5.* Greenwich, CT: JAI Press.

Epstein, J. L., & Dauber, S. L. (1991). School programs and teacher practices of parent involvement in inner-city elementary and middle schools. *The Elementary School Journal, 91,* 289–305.

Epstein, J. L., & Scott-Jones, D. (1988, November). *Accelerating the education for students at risk.* Paper presented at the Invitational Centennial Conference, Stanford, CA.

Erchul, W. P. (1987). A relational communication analysis of control in school consultation. *Professional School Psychology, 2,* 113–124.

Erchul, W. P., & Chewning, T. G. (1990). Behavioral consultation from a request-centered relational communication perspective. *School Psychology Quarterly, 5,* 1–20.

Erchul, W. P., Hughes, J. N., Meyers, J., Hickman, J. A., & Braden, J. P. (1992). Dyadic agreement concerning the consultation process and its relationship to outcome. *Journal of Educational and Psychological Consultation, 3,* 119–132.

Fehrmann, P. G., Keith, T. Z., & Reimers, T. M. (1987). Home influences on school learning: Direct and indirect effects of parent involvement on high school grades. *Journal of Educational Research, 80,* 330–337.

Fine, M. J. (Ed.) (1980). *Handbook on parent education.* New York: Academic Press.

Fine, M. J. (1984). Parent involvement. In J. E. Ysseldyke (Ed.), *School psychology: The state of the art* (pp. 195–224). Minneapolis: National School Psychology Training Network.

Fine, M. J. (1989). *The second handbook on parent education: Contemporaray perspectives.* New York: Academic Press.

Fine, M. J., & Holt, P. (1983). Intervening with school problems: A family systems perspective. *Psychology in the Schools, 20,* 59–66.

Fish, M. C., & Jain, S. (1988). Using systems theory in school assessment and intervention: A structural model for school psychologists. *Professional School Psychology, 3,* 291–300.

Forehand, R., & McMahon, R. J. (1981). *Helping the noncompliant child: A clinician's guide to parent training.* New York: Guilford Press.

Freud, S. (1927). *The ego and the id.* London: Hogarth Press.

Freud, S. (1938). *The basic writings of Sigmund Freud* (A. A. Brill, Ed. and trans.). New York: Random House.

Friedman, R. (1969). A structured family interview in the assessment of school learning disorders. *Psychology in the Schools, 6,* 162–171.

Fuchs, D., & Fuchs, L. S. (1989). Exploring effective and efficient prereferral interventions: A component analysis of behavioral consultation. *School Psychology Review, 18,* 260–283.

Fuchs, D., Fuchs, L. S., & Bahr, M. W. (1990, October–Novermber). Mainstream Assistance Teams: A scientific basis for the art of consultation. *Exceptional Children,* pp. 128–138.

Galloway, J., & Sheridan, S. M. (1994). Implementing scientific practices through case studies: Examples using home–school interventions and consultation. *Journal of School Psychology, 32,* 385–413.

Goldberg, D. (1972). *Manual of the General Health Questionnaire.* Manchester, England: University of Manchester.

Gordon, T. (1975). *P.E.T.: Parent effectiveness training.* New York: American Library.

Gresham, F. M. (1989). Assessment of treatment integrity in school consultation and prereferral intervention. *School Psychology Review, 18,* 37–50.

Gresham, F. M. (1991). Moving beyond statistical significance in reporting consultation outcome research. *Journal of Educational and Psychological Consultation, 2,* 1–13.

Gresham, F. M., & Elliott, S. N. (1990). *The Social Skills Rating System.* Circle Pines, MN: AGS.

Gresham, F. M., & Kendell, G. K. (1987). School consultation research: Methodological critique and future research directions. *School Psychology Review, 16,* 306–316.

Gresham, F., M., & Noell, G. H. (1993). Documenting the effectiveness of consultation outcomes. In J. E. Zins, T. R. Kratochwill, & S. N. Elliott (Eds.), *Handbook of consultation services for children: Applications in educational and clinical settings* (pp. 249-273). San Francisco: JosseyBass.

Grotevant, H. D., & Carlson, C. I. (1989). *Family assessment: A guide to methods and measures.* New York: Guilford Press.

Gump, P. V. (1977). Ecological psychologists: Critics or contributors to behavior analysis. In A. Rogers-Warren & S. F. Warren (Eds.), *Ecological perspectives in behavior analysis* (pp. 133–147). Baltimore: University Park Press.

Gutkin, T. B., & Conoley, J. C. (1990). Reconceptualizing school psychology from a service delivery perspective: Implications for practice, training, and research. *Journal of School Psychology, 28,* 203–223.

Gutkin, T. B., & Curtis, M. J. (1990). School-based consultation: Theory, techniques, and research. In T. B. Gutkin & C. R. Reynolds (Eds.), *The handbook of school psychology* (2nd ed.) (pp. 577–611). New York: Wiley.

Hansen, D. A. (1986). Family–school articulations: The effects of interaction rule mismatch. *American Educational Research Journal, 23,* 643–659.

Harding, J., Wacker, D. P., Cooper, L. J., Millard, T., & Jensen-Kovalan, P. (1994). Brief hierarchical assessment of potential treatment components with children in an outpatient clinic. *Journal of Applied Behavior Analysis, 27,* 291–300.

Hayes, S. C., Nelson, R. O., & Jarrett, R. B. (1986). Evaluating the quality of behavioral assessment. In R. O. Nelson & S. C. Hayes (Eds.), *Conceptual foundations of behavioral assessment* (pp. 463–503). New York: Guilford Press.

Hayes, S. C., Nelson, R. O., & Jarrett, R. B. (1987). The treatment utility of assessment: A functional approach to evaluating assessment quality. *American Psychologist, 42,* 963–974.

Haynes, S. N., & O'Brien, W. H. (1990). Functional analysis in behavior therapy. *Clinical Psychology Review, 10,* 649–668.

Henderson, A. (1987). *The evidence continues to grow: Parent involvement improves student achievement.* Columbia, MD: National Committee for Citizens in Education.

Henderson, A. T., Marburger, C. L., & Ooms, T. (1986). *Beyond the bake sale: An educator's guide to working with parents.* Columbia, MD: National Committee for Citizens in Education.

Hoover-Dempsey, K. V., Bassler, O. C., & Brissie, J. S. (1987). Parent involvement: Contributions of teacher efficacy, school socioeconomic status, and other school characteristics. *American Educational Research Journal, 24*, 417–435.

Horner, R. H. (1994). Functional assessment: Contributions and future directions. *Journal of Applied Behavior Analysis, 27*, 401–404.

Humes, C. W., & Clark, J. N. (1989). Group counseling and consultation with gifted high school students. *Journal for Specialists in Group Work, 14*, 219–225.

Impara, J. C., & Murphy, L. L. (Eds.) (1994). *Psychological assessment in the schools*. Lincoln, NE: Buros Institute of Mental Measurements.

Iwata, B. A., Dorsey, M. F., Slifer, K. J., Bauman, & Richman, G. S. (1982). Toward a functional analysis of self-injury. *Analysis and Intervention in Developmental Disabilities, 2*, 3–20.

Jackson, R. M., Cleveland, J. C., & Merenda, P. F. (1975). The longitudinal effects of early identification and counseling of underachievers. *Journal of School Psychology, 13*, 119–128.

Jenson, W. R., Rhode, G., & Reavis, H. K. (in press). What, me worry? Practical solutions to everyday parenting problems. Longmont, CO: Sopris-West.

Jowett, S., & Baginsky, M. (1988). Parents and education: A survey of their involvement and discussion of some issues. *Educational Research, 30*, 36–45.

Kanfer, F. H., & Goldstein, A. P. (Eds.) (1986). *Helping people change: A textbook of methods*. New York: Pergamon Press.

Kaufman, A. S., & Kaufman, N. L. (1990). *Kaufman's brief Intelligence Test (K-BIT)*. Circle Pines, MN: AGS.

Kazdin, A. E. (1977). Assessing the clinical or applied importance of behavior change through social validation. *Behavior Modification, 1*, 427–452.

Kazdin, A. E. (1981). Acceptability of child treatment techniques: The influence of treatment efficacy and adverse side effects. *Behavior Therapy, 12*, 493–506.

Kazdin, A. E. (1982). Symptom substitution, generalization, and response covariation: Implications for psychotherapy outcome. *Psychological Bulletin, 91*, 349–365.

Kazdin, A. E. (1994). *Behavior modification in applied settings* (5th ed.). Pacific Grove, CA: Brooks/Cole.

Knoff, H. M. (1984). The practice of multimodal consultation: An integrating approach for consultation service delivery. *Psychology in the Schools, 21*, 83–91.

Kovacs, M. (1980). Rating scales to assess depression in school aged children. *Acta Paedopsychiatrica, 46*, 305–315.

Kramer, J. J. (1990a). Best practices in parent training. In A. T. Thomas & J. Grimes (Eds.), *Best practices in school psychology-II* (pp. 263–273). Washington, DC: National Association of School Psychologists.

Kramer, J. J. (1990b). Training parents as behavior change agents: Successes, failures, and suggestions for school psychologists. In T. B. Gutkin & C. R. Reynolds (Eds.), *The handbook of school psychology* (2nd ed.) (pp. 683–702). New York: Wiley.

Kratochwill, T. R. (1985). Case study research in school psychology. *School Psychology Review, 14*, 204–215.

Kratochwill, T. R., & Bergan, J. R. (1990). *Behavioral consultation in applied settings: An individual guide*. New York: Plenum Press.

Kratochwill, T. R., & Sheridan, S. M. (1990). Advances in behavioral assessment. In C. R. Reynolds & T. B. Gutkin (Eds.), *Handbook of school psychology* (2nd ed.) (pp. 328–364). New York: Wiley.

Kratochwill, T. R., Sheridan, S. M., & Van Someren, K. R. (1988). Research in behavioral consultation: Current status and future directions. In F. West (Ed.), *School consultation: Interdisciplinary perspectives on theory, research, training, and practice* (pp. 77–102). Austin, TX: University of Texas Press.

Lalli, J. S., Browder, D. M., Mace, F. C., & Brow, D. K. (1993). Teacher use of descriptive analysis data to implement interventions to decrease students' problem behaviors. *Journal of Applied Behavior Analysis, 26*, 227–238.

Lentz, F. E., & Shapiro, E. S. (1986). Functional assessment of the academic environment. *School Psychology Review, 15*, 346–357.

Lewis, T. J., Scott, T. M., & Sugai, G. (1994). The Problem Behavior Questionnaire: A teacher based instrument to develop functional hypotheses of problem behvaior in general education classrooms. *Diagnostique,19*, (2–3), 103–115.

Mace, F. C., Lalli, J. S., & Pinter-Lalli, E. (1991). Functional analysis and treatment of aberrant behavior. *Research in Developmental Disabilities, 12*, 155–180.

Mannino, F. V., & Shore, M. F. (1975). The effects of consultation: A review of the literature. *American Journal of Community Psychology, 3*, 1–21.

Martens, B. K. (1993). A behavioral approach to consultation. In J. E. Zins, T. R. Kratochwill, & S. N. Elliott (Eds.), *Handbook of consultation services for children: Applications in educational and clinical settings* (pp. 65–86). San Francisco, CA: Jossey-Bass.

Martens, B. K., Lewandowski, L. J., & Houk, J. L. (1989). Correlational analysis of verbal interactions during the consultative interview and consultees' subsequent perceptions. *Professional Psychology: Research and Practice, 20*, 334–339.

McCubbin, H., Larsen, A. S., & Olson, D. H. (1982). *Family Crisis Oriented Personal Scales (F-COPES)*. University of Minnesota, Department of Family Social Science.

McDaniel, S. (1981). Treating school problems in family therapy. *Elementary School Guidance and Counseling, 15*, 214–222.

McGinnis, E., & Goldstein, A. P. (1984). *Skillstreaming the elementary school child: A guide for teaching prosocial skills*. Champaign, IL: Research Press.

Medway, F. J. (1979). How effective is school consultation? A review of recent research. *Journal of School Psychology, 17*, 275–282.

Medway, F. J. (1982). School consultation research; Past trends and future directions. *Professional Psychology, 13*, 422–430.

Medway, F. J. (1989). Measuring the effectiveness of parent education. In M. J. Fine (Ed.), *The second handbook on parent education: Contemporary perspectives* (pp. 237–255). New York: Academic Press.

Medway, F. J., & Updyke, J. F. (1985). Meta-analysis of consultation outcome studies. *American Journal of Community Psychology, 13*, 489–505.

Merrell, K. W. (1993). *School Social Behavior Scales*. Bradon, VT: Clinical Psychology Publishing Co.

Milne, A. M., Myers, D. E., Rosenthal, A. S., & Ginsburg, A. (1986). Single parents, working mothers, and the educational achievement of school children. *Sociology of Education, 59,* 125–139.

Milner, J. S. (1980). *The Child Abuse Potential Inventory.* Webster, NC: Psychtec Corp.

Minuchin, S. (1974). *Families and family therapy.* Cambridge, MA: Harvard University Press.

Minuchin, S., & Fishman, H. (1981). *Family therapy techniques.* Cambridge, MA: Harvard University Press.

Moos, R. H. (1974). *The Family, Work, & Group Environment Scales Manual.* Palo Alto, CA: Consulting Psychologists Press.

Moreland, J. R., Schwebel, A. I., Beck, S., & Wells, R. (1982). Parents as therapists: A review of the behavior therapy parent training literature — 1975 to 1981. *Behavior Modification, 6,* 250–276.

Natriello, G., McDill, E. L., & Pallas, A. M. (1990). *Schooling disadvantaged children: Racing against catastrophe.* New York: Teachers College Press, Columbia University.

Neef, N. A., & Iwata, B. A. (1994). Current research on functional analysis methodologies: An introduction. *Journal of Applied Behavior Analysis, 27,* 211–214.

Nelson, R. O. (1983). Behavioral assessment: Past, present, and future. *Behavioral Assessment, 5,* 195–206.

Northup, J., Wacker, D., Sasso, G., Steege, M., Cigrand, K., Cook, J., & DeRaad, A. (1991). A brief functional analysis of aggressive and alternative behavior in an outpatient setting. *Journal of Applied Behavior Analysis, 24,* 509–522.

Nye, B. A. (1989). Effective parent education and involvement models and programs: Contemporary strategies for school implementation. In M. J. Fine (Ed.), *The second handbook on parent education: Contemporary perspectives* (pp. 325–345). New York: Academic Press.

Olson, D. H., Portner, J., & Lavee, Y. (1985). *Family Adaptability and Cohesion Evaluation Scales III (FACES III).* University of Minnesota, Department of Family Social Science.

O'Neill, R. E., Horner, R. H., Albin, R. W., Storey, K., & Sprague, J. R. (1990). *Functional analysis of problem behavior: A practical assessment guide.* Sycamore, IL: Sycamore Publishing Co.

Paget, K. D. (1987). Systemic family assessment: Concepts and strategies for school psychologists. *School Psychology Review, 16,* 429–442.

Palmo, A. J., & Kuzinar, J. (1972). Modification of behavior through group counseling and consultation. *Elementary School Guidance and Counseling, 6,* 258–262.

Patterson, G. R., & Reid, J. G. (1973). Intervention for families of aggressive boys: A replication study. *Behavior Research and Therapy, 11,* 383–394.

Patterson, G. R., Reid, J. G., Jones, R. R., & Conger, R. E. (1975). *A social learning approach to family intervention.* Eugene, OR: Castalia Press.

Petrie, P., Brown, K. D., Piersel, W. C., Frinrock, S. R., Schelble, M., Leblanc, C. P., & Kratochwill, T. R. (1980). The school psychologist as behavioral ecologist. *Journal of School Psychology, 18,* 222–223.

Piersel, W. C., & Kratochwill, T. R. (1979). Self-observation and behavior change: Applications to academic and adjustment problems through behavioral consultation. *Journal of School Psychology, 17,* 151–161.

Piersel, W. C., & Kratochwill, T. R. (1981). A teacher-implemented contingency management package to assess and treat selective mutism. *Behavioral Assessment, 3,* 371–382.

Plunge, M., Waters-Guetschow, K., Kratochwill, T. R., & Gettinger, M. (1995). Parent advocacy: Making the assessment and intervention process user friendly. In M. Breen & C. Fiedler (Eds.), *Behavioral approach to the assessment of emotionally disturbed youth: A handbook for school-based practitioners* (pp. xx-xx). Austin, TX: Pro-Ed.

Popkin, M. H. (1983). *Active parenting.* Atlanta: Active Parenting.

Power, T. J. (1985). Perceptions of competence: How parents and teachers view each other. *Psychology in the Schools, 22,* 68–78.

Power, T. J., & Bartholomew, K. L. (1985). Getting uncaught in the middle: A case study in family–school system consultation. *School Psychology Review, 16,* 498–512.

Power, T. J., & Bartholomew, K. L. (1987). Family–school relationship patterns: An ecological assessment. *School Psychology Review, 16,* 498–512.

Pray, B., Kramer, J. J., & Lindskog, R. (1986). Assessment and treatment of tic behavior: A review and case study. *School Psychology Review, 15,* 418–429.

Procidiano, M. W., & Heller, K. (1983). Measures of perceived social support from friends and from family: Three validation studies. *American Journal of Community Psychology, 11,* 1–25.

Quay, H. C., & Peterson, D. R. (1983). *Manual for the Revised Behavior Problem Checklist.* Coral Gables, FL: Applied Social Sciences, University of Miami.

Repp, A. (1994). Comments on functional analysis procedures for school-based behavior problems. *Journal of Applied Behavior Analysis, 27,* 409–411.

Reynolds, C. R., & Richmond, B. O. (1985). *The Revised Children's Manifest Anxiety Scale (RCMAS): What I think and feel.* Los Angeles, CA: Western Psychological Services.

Reynolds, W. (1986). *Reynolds Adolescent Depression Scale: Professional manual.* Odessa, FL: Psychological Assessment Resources, Inc.

Reynolds, W. M. (1989). *Reynolds Child Depression Scale: Professional manual.* Odessa, FL: Psychological Assessment Resources, Inc.

Rogers-Warren, A., & Warren, S. F. (Eds.). (1977). *Ecological perspectives in behavior analysis.* Baltimore: University Park Press.

Rosenfield, S. A., & Gravois, T. (1995). *Instructional consultation teams: Collaborating for change.* New York: Guilford Press.

Sanders, M. R., & Dadds, M. R. (1993). *Behavioral family intervention.* Boston: Allyn & Bacon.

Sasso, G. M., Reimers, T. M., Cooper, L. J., Wacker, D., Berg, W., Steege, M., Kelly, L., & Allaire, A. (1992). Use of descriptive and experimental analysis to identify the functional properties of aberrant behavior in school settings. *Journal of Applied Behavior Analysis, 25,* 809–821.

Scherer, M. W., & Nakamura, C. Y. (1968). A fear survey schedule for children (FSS-FC): An analytic comparison with manifest anxiety. *Behavior Research and Therapy, 6,* 173–182.

Sheridan, S. M. (1992). Consultant and client outcomes of competency-based behavioral consultation training. *School Psychology Quarterly, 7,* 1–26.

Sheridan, S. M. (1993). Parent consultation: Current trends and future directions. In J. E. Zins, T. R. Kratochwill, & S. N. Elliott (Eds.), *The handbook of consultation services for children:*

Applications in educational and clinical settings (pp. 110–133). San Francisco: Jossey-Bass.

Sheridan, S. M. (1994, August). Conceptual and empirical bases of conjoint behavioral consultation. Invited address presented at the Annual Meeting of the American Psychological Association, Los Angeles, CA.

Sheridan, S. M., & Colton, D. L. (1994). Conjoint behavioral consultation: A review and case study. *Journal of Educational and Psychological Consultation, 5*, 211–228.

Sheridan, S. M., & Dee, C. C. (in preparation). *Social skills for the tough kid: A program for parents.* Longmont, CO: Sopris-West.

Sheridan, S. M., & Kratochwill, T. R. (1991). Behavioral consultation in applied settings. In J. W. Lloyd, A. C. Repp, & N. N. Singh (Eds.), *The regular education initiative: Alternative perspectives on concepts, issues, and methods* (pp. 193–210). Sycamore, IL: Sycamore Publishing Co.

Sheridan, S. M., & Kratochwill, T. R. (1992). Behavioral parent–teacher consultation: Conceptual and research considerations. *Journal of School Psychology, 30*, 117–139.

Sheridan, S. M., Kratochwill, T. R., & Elliott, S. N. (1990). Behavioral consultation with parents and teachers: Delivering treatment for socially withdrawn children at home and school. *School Psychology Review, 19*, 33–52.

Sheridan, S. M., Kratochwill, T. R., & Ramirez, S. (1995). Diagnosis and treatment of elective mutism: Recommendations and a case study. *Special Services in the Schools.*

Sheridan, S. M., & Steck, M. (1995). Acceptability of conjoint behavioral consultation: A national survey of school psychologists. *School Psychology Review.*

Sibley, S. (1986). A meta-analysis of school consultation research. Unpublished doctoral dissertation. Denton, TX: Texas Woman's University.

Spanier, G. B. (1976). Measuring dyadic adjustment: New scales for assessing marital quality. *Journal of Marriage and the Family, 38*, 15–28.

Spielberger, C. D., Gorsuch, R. C., & Lushene, R. E. (1970). *Manual for the State–Trait Anxiety Inventory.* Palo Alto, CA: Consulting Psychologists Press.

Stevenson, D. L., & Baker, D. P. (1987). The family–school relation and the child's school performance. *Child Development, 58*, 1348–1357.

Strother, J., & Jacobs, E. (1986). Parent consultation: A practical approach. *The School Counselor, 33*, 292–296.

Swap, S. M. (1993). *Developing home–school partnerships: From concepts to practice.* New York: Teachers College Press.

Taverne, A., & Sheridan, S. M. (1995). Parent training in interactive book reading: An investigation of its effects with families at risk. *School Psychology Quarterly, 10*, 41–64.

Tawney, J. W., & Gast, D. L. (1984). *Single subject research in special education.* Columbus, OH: Merrill.

Taylor, J. C., & Romanczyk, R. G. (1994). Generating hypotheses about the function of student problem behavior by observing teacher behavior. *Journal of Applied Behavior Analysis, 27*, 251–265.

Tombari, M., & Bergan, J. (1978). Consultant cues and teacher verbalizations, judgments, and expectancies concerning children's adjustment problems. *Journal of School Psychology, 16*, 212–219.

Tunnecliffe, M. R., Leach, D. J., & Tunnecliffe, L. P. (1986). Relative efficacy of using behavioral consultation as an approach to teacher stress management. *Journal of School Psychology*, *24*, 123–131.

Twernbold, M. A., Kratochwill, T. R., & Gardner, W. I. (in press). Behavioral-oriented assessment: Conducting a functional analysis of behavior. In M. Breen & C. Fiedler (Eds.), *Behavioral approach to the assessment of emotionally disturbed youth: A handbook for school-based practitioners* (pp.). Austin, TX: Pro-Ed.

Von Brock, M. B., & Elliott, S. N. (1987). Influence of treatment effectiveness information on the acceptability of classroom interventions. *Journal of School Psychology*, *25*, 131–144.

Wacker, D. P., Berg, W. K., Cooper, L. J., Derby, M., Steege, M. W., Northup, J., & Sasso, G. (1994). The impact of functional analysis methodology on outpatient clinic services. *Journal of Applied Behavior Analysis*, *27*, 405–407.

Wahler, R. G., & Fox, J. J. (1981). Setting events in applied behavior analysis: Toward a conceptual and methodological expansion. *Journal of Applied Behavior Analysis*, *14*, 327–338.

Walker, H. M., & McConnell, S. R. (1988). *The Walker–McConnell Scale of Social Competence and School Adjustment*. Austin, TX: Pro-Ed.

Wang, M. C., Gennari, P., & Waxman, H. C. (1985). The Adaptive Learning Environment Model: Design, implementation, and effects. In M. C. Wang & H. J. Walberg (Eds.), *Adapting instruction to individual differences* (pp. 121–235). Berkeley, CA: McCutchen.

Webster-Stratton, C. (1987). *Parents and children: A 10 program videotape parent training series with manuals*. Eugene, OR: Castalia Press.

Webster-Stratton, C. (1990). Enhancing the effectiveness of self-administered videotape parent training for families with conduct-problem children. *Journal of Abnormal Child Psychology*, *18*, 479–492.

Webster-Stratton, C., Hollinsworth, T., & Kolpacoff, M. (1989). The long-term effectiveness and clinical significance of three cost-effective training programs for families with conduct-problem children. *Journal of Consulting and Clinical Psychology*, *57*, 550–553.

Weise, M. J. (1989). Evaluation of an Adlerian parent training program with multiple outcome measures. Unpublished doctoral dissertation. University of Nebraska-Lincoln.

Welch, M., & Sheridan, S. M. (1995). *Educational partnerships: Serving students at risk*. San Antonio, TX: Harcourt Brace.

Wickstrom, K. F., & Witt, J. C. (1993). Resistance within school-based consultation. In J. E. Zins, T. R. Kratochwill, & S. N. Elliott (Eds.), *Handbook of consultation services for children* (pp. 159–178). San Francisco: Jossey-Bass.

Witt, J. C., & Elliott, S. N. (1985). Acceptability of classroom intervention strategies. In T. R. Kratochwill (Ed.), *Advances in school psychology* (Vol. 4); (pp. 251–288). Hillsdale, NJ: Lawrence Erlbaum.

Witt, J. C., & Martens, B. K. (1988). Problems with problem-solving consultation: A re-analysis of assumptions, methods, and goals. *School Psychology Review*, *17*, 211–226.

Witt, J. C., Martens, B. K., & Elliott, S. N. (1984). Factors affecting teachers' judgments of the acceptability of behavioral interventions: Time involvement, behavior problem severity, and type of intervention. *Behavior Therapy*, *15*, 204–209.

Woodcock, R. W., & Mather, N. (1990). *Woodcock-Johnson Psychoeducational Battery-Revised*. Allen, TX: DLM Teaching Resources.

Wright, L. (1976). Indirect treatment of children through principle-oriented parent consultation. *Journal of Consulting and Clinical Psychology, 44,* 148.

Ysseldyke, J. E., & Christenson, S. L. (1987). *The Instructional Environment Scale (TIES).* Austin, TX: Pro-Ed.

Appendix

Conjoint Behavioral
Consultation Interview Forms

Conjoint Problem Identification Interview (CPII)

Child's Name: _____   Date: _____

Parent's Name: _____   Age: _____

Teacher's Name: _____   Grade: _____

School: _____

Consultant's Name: _____

Consultant's Note: The goals of the CPII are to:

- Establish a working relationship between parents and teacher and between the consultant and consultees.

- Define the problem(s) in behavioral terms.

- Provide a tentative identification of behavior in terms of antecedent, situation, and consequent conditions across settings.

- Provide a tentative strength of the behavior across settings (e.g., how often or severe).

- Discuss and reach agreement on a goal for behavior change across settings.

- Establish a procedure for collecting baseline data across settings in terms of sampling plan, what is to be recorded, who is to record the data, and how the behavior is to be recorded.

CPII (*Continued*)

The consultant should question and/or comment on all of the following:

OPENING SALUTATION

GENERAL STATEMENT TO OPEN CONSULTATION

What seems to be the problem? What is it that you are concerned about?

Home   School

BEHAVIOR SPECIFICATION

a. Tell me what you mean by...Give me some specific examples of what you mean by...What does the child do?

Home   School

b. What are some more examples?

Home   School

(*Continued*)

CPII (*Continued*)

c. We've discussed several behaviors, such as... Which of these is most problematic across settings? — *Prioritize one or two behaviors to target across settings.*

Home   School

TARGET BEHAVIOR DEFINITION

Let's define exactly what we mean by...What would be a good definition of...?

Summarize Target Behavior in Precise, Observable Terms

HISTORY OF PROBLEM

Approximately when did this specific problem begin? How long has this been a problem?

CPII (*Continued*)

BEHAVIOR SETTING

a. Where does the child display this target behavior? Give me some examples of where this occurs.

       Home   School

b. What are some more examples of where this specific behavior occurs?

       Home   School

c. Which of the settings at school is most problematic? Which of the settings at home is most problematic? — *Establish one setting priority at home and one at school.*

       Home   School

(Continued)

CPII (*Continued*)

CONDITIONAL/FUNCTIONAL ANALYSIS

                                          Home   School

Antecedent Conditions and Setting Events
What typically happens at home/school
before the behavior occurs?

What is a typical morning like before your
child goes to school?

What events occur earlier in the day (in
other settings or times of the day) that
might affect the child's behavior?

Consequent Conditions
What typically happens at home/school
after the behavior occurs?

How are school-related behavior problems
handled at home?

Environmental/Sequential Conditions
What else is typically happening at
home/school when the behavior occurs?

What time of day or day of week is the
behavior most/least likely to occur?

What activities are most/least likely to
produce the behavior?

With whom are the behaviors most/least
likely to occur?

How many other people are in the setting
when the behavior is most likely to occur?

CPII (*Continued*)

CONDITIONAL/FUNCTIONAL ANALYSIS (*continued*)

Home   School

Environmental/Sequential Conditions
    What are some other particular situations
    that might "set off" the behavior?

    What other events (e.g., medications,
    medical complications, routines) may
    affect the behavior?

Summarize/Validate Conditions and Functions of the Behavior

BEHAVIOR STRENGTH ACROSS SETTINGS

How often does this behavior occur at home/at school? How long does
it last?

Home   School

Summarize/Validate the Specific Behavior and Its Strength

GOAL OF CONSULTATION

What would be an acceptable level of this behavior at home/at school?
What would the child have to do to get along OK? Is there general
agreement of our goal across home and school?

Home   School

CPII (*Continued*)

EXISTING PROCEDURES

What are some programs or procedures that are currently operating in the classroom? How are problems currently dealt with when the occur at home/at school?

Home   School

CHILD'S STRENGTHS/ASSETS

What are some of the things that the child is good at? What are some of the child's strengths?

POSSIBLE REINFORCERS

What are some things (events, activities, etc.) that the child finds reinforcing? What are some things the child likes to do?

Summarize/Validate Behavior, Strength, Goal, etc.

RATIONALE FOR DATA COLLECTION

It would be very helpful to watch the behavior for a week or so and monitor its occurrence. This will help us key in on some important facts that we may have missed, and also help us document the progress that is made towards our goal.

CPII (*Continued*)

CROSS-SETTING DATA COLLECTION PROCEDURES

What would be a simple way for you to keep track of the behavior at home/at school?)

        Home   School

Summarize/Validate Data Collection Procedures

DATE TO BEGIN DATA COLLECTION

When can you begin to collect data at home/at school?

        Home   School

NEXT APPOINTMENT

When can we all get together again to discuss the data and determine where to go from here?

CLOSING SALUTATION

Conjoint Problem Analysis Interview (CPAI)

Child's Name: _____ Date: _____

Parent's Name: _____ Age: _____

Teacher's Name: _____ Grade: _____

School: _____

Consultant's Name:_____

Consultant's Note: The goals of the CPAI are to:

- Evaluate and obtain agreement on the sufficiency and adequacy of baseline data across settings.

- Conduct a functional analysis of the behavior across settings (i.e., discuss antecedent, consequent, and sequential conditions).

- Identify setting events (events that are functionally related, but temporally or contextually distal to the target behavior), ecological conditions, and other cross-setting variables that may impact the target behavior.

CPAI (*Continued*)

The consultant should question and/or comment on the following:

OPENING SALUTATION

GENERAL STATEMENT REGARDING DATA AND PROBLEM

Were you able to keep a record of the behavior?

        Home   School

BEHAVIOR STRENGTH ACROSS SETTINGS

According to the data, it looks like the behavior occurred_____at home/at school) — *Record data here.*

        Home   School

ANTECEDENT CONDITIONS

What did you notice before the problem occurred at home/at school? What things may have led up to its occurrence? What happened before school on these days? — *Refer to baseline data!*

        Home   School

(Continued)

CPAI (*Continued*)

CONSEQUENT CONDITIONS

What typically happened after the occurrence of the behavior at home/at school? What types of things did you notice afterward that may have maintained its occurrence? What happened after school on these days? — *Refer to baseline data!*

Home   School

SEQUENTIAL CONDITIONS

What else was happening in the classroom/playground/home when the behavior occurred? What time of day or day of week seemed most problematic at home/at school? What patterns did you notice in the child's behavior at home/at school?

Home   School

Summarize/Validate Behavior/Strength/Conditions

CPAI (*Continued*)

BEHAVIOR INTERPRETATION

Why do you think the child does this? It sounds like the behavior might also be related to...

Home   School

CROSS-SETTING PLAN DEVELOPMENT

It seems that we need to try something different. What can be done at both home and school to reach our goal? — *A written plan for teacher and parents may be helpful.*

Home   School

Summarize/Validate Plan Across Settings

(Continued)

CPAI (*Continued*)

DATA RECORDING PROCEDURES

It would be very helpful if we could continue to collect data on the child's behavior. Can we continue the same recording procedure as before?

Home   School

NEXT APPOINTMENT

When can we all get together again to discuss the data and determine where to go from here?

CLOSING SALUTATION

Conjoint Treatment Evaluation Interview (CTEI)

Child's Name: _____ Date: _____

Parent's Name: _____ Age: _____

Teacher's Name: _____ Grade: _____

School: _____

Consultant's Name: _____

Consultant's Note: The goals of the CTEI are to:

■ Determine whether the goals of consultation have been attained across settings.

■ Evaluate the effectiveness of the treatment plan across settings.

■ Discuss strategies and tactics regarding the continuation, modification, or termination of the treatment plan.

■ Schedule additional interviews if necessary, or terminate consultation.

CTEI (*Continued*)

The consultant should question and/or comment on all of the following:

OPENING SALUTATION

GENERAL PROCEDURES AND OUTCOME

How did things go with the plan? — *Record treatment data here.*

        Home   School

GOAL ATTAINMENT ACROSS SETTINGS

Has the goal been met at home/at school?

        Home   School

CTEI (*Continued*)

If goals have <u>not</u> been attained, discuss:

PLAN MODIFICATIONS

How can we modify the procedures so that the plan is more effective at home and school?

              Home   School

NEXT APPOINTMENT

When can we meet again to discuss the effectiveness of our new or modified plan?

If goals <u>have</u> been attained, discuss:

PLAN EFFECTIVENESS ACROSS SETTINGS

Do you think that the *behavioral program* was responsible for the child's change in behavior?

              Home   School

(Continued)

CTEI (*Continued*)

EXTERNAL VALIDITY OF PLAN

Do you think this plan would work with another child with similar difficulties?

            Home   School

POST-IMPLEMENTATION PLANNING

Should we leave the plan in effect for a while longer?

            Home   School

PROCEDURES FOR GENERALIZATION/MAINTENANCE

How can we encourage the child to display these behavior changes in other settings or with other behaviors? What procedures should we use to make sure that the behavior change continues over time?

            Home   School

CTEI (*Continued*)

FOLLOW-UP ASSESSMENT PROCEDURES

How can we monitor the child's progress to ensure that these positive changes continue?

Home   School

NEED FOR FUTURE INTERVIEWS

Would you like to meet again to check the child's progress?

Home   School

TERMINATION OF CONSULTATION (if appropriate)

CLOSING SALUTATION

About the Authors and Contributors

Susan M. Sheridan received her Ph.D. in Educational Psychology from the University of Wisconsin–Madison in 1989, with a specialization in School Psychology. She is currently an Associate Professor in Educational Psychology at the University of Utah. Dr. Sheridan was bestowed the 1993 Lightner Witmer Award for early career accomplishments by Division 16 of the American Psychological Association, and the Outstanding Young Graduate Award from the School of Education at the University of Wisconsin. She is the author of over 30 articles, 15 book chapters, and 3 books. She also has conducted over 50 professional presentations in the areas of consultation, collaboration, and social skills. Her primary interests are in conjoint behavioral consultation, interdisciplinary collaboration, home–school partnerships, and social skills interventions.

Thomas R. Kratochwill received his Ph.D. in Educational Psychology from the University of Wisconsin–Madison in 1973, with a specialization in School Psychology. His is currently a Professor in Educational Psychology and Director of the School Psychology Program at the University of Wisconsin–Madison. Dr. Kratochwill received the Lightner Witmer Award from Division 16 of the American Psychological Association, and in 1995 he received the Senior Scientist Award from the Division. He is the author of over 100 journal articles, book chapters, and monographs. He has written or edited 20 books and has made over 100 presentations at professional meetings. Dr. Kratochwill's research and professional writing has focused primarily of behavioral consultation and therapy, internalizing disorders of children, single subject methodology in applied and clinical research, and professional issues in school psychology.

JOHN R. BERGAN received his Ph.D. in Education and Psychology from the University of Michigan. He is currently Professor Emeritus of Educational Psychology at the University of Arizona and is President of Assessment Technology Incorporated. Dr. Bergan is the author of over 70 publications, including books, chapters, and journal articles focusing on consultation and measurement issues related to the cognitive and social development of young children. In 1981, Dr. Bergan received the Distinguished Psychologist Award from the Arizona State Psychological Association, and in 1982, the Presidential Citation from the National Child Care Association. His primary research interests are in the areas of behavioral consultation and measurement.

*   *   *   *

DENISE COLTON received her M.S. degree from the University of Utah and is currently a doctoral candidate in the Department of Educational Psychology, with a specialization in School Psychology. Her interests are in the areas of conjoint behavioral consultation, inclusion, and students with Attention Deficit Hyperactivity Disorder.

JOANN GALLOWAY received her Ph.D. in Educational Psychology from the University of Utah in 1992, with a specialization in School Psychology. She is currently a Certified School Psychologist in Sandy, Utah. Her interests are in the areas of behavioral consultation with preschool and elementary populations, and interventions aimed at improving children's social competence.

SHERRY ROBERTSON received her M.S. degree in School Psychology from the University of Wisconsin–Madison and is currently a doctoral candidate in the Department of Educational Psychology, with a specialization in School Psychology. She is presently the project coordinator and consultant for a federal grant that provides consultation services to parents and teachers of Head Start students. Her research and writing interests include behavioral consultation in the schools, child and family therapy, and Goal Attainment Scaling.

INGRID SLADECZEK received her Ph.D. in Psychology from the University of Arizona and specialized in School Psychology at the University of Wisconsin–Madison. She is currently an Assistant Professor on Educational and Counselling Psychology at McGill University. Her research and writing interests include behavioral consultation and therapy in the schools, child and adolescent psychhopathology, and research methodology.

Index